THE LIMITS OF GOVERNMENT REGULATION

THE LIMITS OF GOVERNMENT REGULATION

EDITED BY

James F. Gatti

School of Business Administration
University of Vermont
Burlington, Vermont

With a Foreword by Malcolm F. Severance

1981
ACADEMIC PRESS
A Subsidiary of Harcourt Brace Jovanovich, Publishers
New York London Toronto Sydney San Francisco

ACADEMIC PRESS, INC.
111 Fifth Avenue, New York, New York 10003

United Kingdom Edition published by
ACADEMIC PRESS, INC. (LONDON) LTD.
24/28 Oval Road, London NW1 7DX

Library of Congress Cataloging in Publication Data
Main entry under title:

The Limits of government regulation.

Includes bibliographical references.
Contents: An overview of the problem of government regulation / James F. Gatti -- Government regulation and a free society / William E. Simon -- A new threat to freedom: the challenge of the 1980's / Harry J. Bolwell -- [etc.]
1. Industry and state--United States--Addresses, essays, lectures. 2. Industry and state--Addresses, essays, lectures. 3. Economic policy--Addresses, essays, lectures. I. Gatti, James F.

HD3616.U47L497 338.973 81-12858
ISBN 0-12-277620-8 (Cloth) AACR2
ISBN 0-12-277622-4 (Paper)

PRINTED IN THE UNITED STATES OF AMERICA

81 82 83 84 9 8 7 6 5 4 3 2 1

To my father and the memory of my mother:
My debt to them is more than can ever be repaid.

Contents

List of Contributors

Numbers in parentheses indicate the pages on which the contributions begin.

ARTHUR ANDERSEN & Co. (95), 1345 Avenue of the Americas, New York, New York 10105

HARRY J. BOLWELL (25), Midland-Ross Corporation, 20600 Chagrin Boulevard, Cleveland, Ohio 44122

ALLEN R. FERGUSON (143), Public Interest Economics Center, 1525 New Hampshire Avenue, N.W., Washington, D.C. 20036

JAMES F. GATTI (1, 167), School of Business Administration, University of Vermont, Burlington, Vermont 05405

THOMAS A. MURPHY (133), General Motors Corporation, General Motors Building, Detroit, Michigan 48233

JOHN O'SULLIVAN (59), *Policy Review*, 513 C Street, N.E., Washington, D.C. 20002

WILLIAM E. SIMON (11), 505 Park Avenue, New York, New York 10022

THOMAS SOWELL (35), Hoover Institution, Stanford University, Stanford, California 94305

THE BUSINESS ROUNDTABLE (95), 200 Park Avenue, New York, New York, 10166
MURRAY L. WEIDENBAUM (87, 143), Council of Economic Advisers, 17th and Pennsylvania Avenue, N.W., Washington, D.C. 20500

Foreword

The regulation of private economic activity by all levels of government has become a cause for growing concern in the United States and, indeed, in most of the capitalist world. There is a perception in some quarters that the pervasiveness of this intervention has reached a point where it may be imposing a substantial drag on social as well as economic progress.

In an attempt to foster meaningful discussion and debate on this problem, the School of Business Administration at the University of Vermont (UVM) began to sponsor a series of lectures on government regulation in the spring of 1979. The series took the form of seminars presented by distinguished members of the academic, business, and government communities who had become involved in a variety of ways with the regulatory process. Their experiences varied from scientific research into the costs and benefits of public sector activity, to actual implementation of regulatory directives, to operating under those rules. Their common ground was, and is, a sincere wish to move the debate from the partisan political arena to the more objective forum of open public debate. The series has provided the students at UVM with a unique opportunity to share, in person, the insights of the invited guests and to learn by challenging their positions. This volume is a compendium of those lectures given during the 1979–1980 academic year.

Though thanks are due many, many people, foremost among them is John Beckley, UVM '34. Without his generosity, encouragement, and laissez-faire attitude toward program design, the seminar series would never have achieved as much as it has. He has our enduring gratitude.

Special thanks go to two participant's whose remarks unfortunately were unavailable for publication, but whose contributions were, nonetheless, substantial: Hon. Richard A. Snelling, Governor of Vermont, and David Lawrence, Manager—Civil Business Analysis, Sikorsky Aircraft. Governor Snelling initiated the series in the spring of 1979 with a talk entitled "Government Regulation: The Dilemma of the Public Official." A successful entrepreneur before election to public office, his remarks brought a unique perspective to the problem. David Lawrence's comments concerning the impact of airline regulation on technological innovation in the industry were exceptionally timely coming as they did in the midst of the dismantling of the CAB.

We would also like to express our gratitude to Arthur Andersen & Co. and The Business Roundtable for their permission to use excerpts from their *Cost of Government Regulation Study*. We hope that their work will provide a basis and methodology for others to improve our understanding of the extent of the regulatory burden. In connection with this study, special thanks go to H. Kendall Hobbs, an audit partner at Arthur Andersen & Co. He gave generously of his time and expertise in explaining and analyzing the study at one of the seminars at UVM. We were far better informed for his efforts.

As head of the business program, I am indebted to my colleagues E. Lauck Parke, who assumed responsibility for the program for the fall semester, and James F. Gatti, who planned and executed the program for the spring. D. Jacque Grinnell and Gene Laber contributed valuable suggestions during the planning process. Particular accolades go to James F. Gatti, who has assembled the materials, organized the manuscript, and performed the essential and demanding task of editing. Countless hours were willingly and cheerfully contributed by our talented secretaries Lynn Wells and Susanna Bouvier. Without their diligence, this volume would not have been possible. We hope the contents will provide the reader with the same valuable insights gained by the students and faculty at the University as we addressed the issues of regulation in the present society.

MALCOLM F. SEVERANCE
School of Business Administration
University of Vermont

Preface

This book is a collection of nine essays addressing the current controversy over the costs and benefits of government regulation of economic activity and the issues involved in developing and implementing such policies. The views of all but one of the authors can be fairly described as neoconservative in principle; however, none would go so far as to reject out-of-hand all collective restrictions on private actions. Furthermore, while their individualistic philosophies would certainly lead them to prefer an anarchic utopia over its collective counterpart, their practicality requires that they acknowledge the fact that there are circumstances in which the unfettered free market solution can be improved upon by means of government intervention.

From their perspectives, there are two basic problems in the current structure of public sector regulation. First, they argue that even where a laissez-faire solution is not optimal, it is superior to the alternatives. In this respect they feel that government policy has erred by attempting to achieve perfection and in the process has replaced private errors with those of the public sector bureaucrat. Their second point (and in this matter all authors are in agreement) is that even where intervention could improve the market solution, the actual policies used have suffered from the fatal mistake of attempting to repeal rather than use the basic market forces to attain the desired result. It is as if manned flight were attempted by denying that the force of gravity should exist rather than using the basic laws of physics to design an aircraft.

A SUMMARY OF THE PAPERS

Following an introductory chapter by James F. Gatti, William E. Simon and Harry J. Bolwell open Part I with individual essays that call for a reassessment of governmental policy on the basis of its impact on our real standard of living and personal freedom. From Simon's perspective as a participant in the financial markets, inflation gets top billing as a threat to the long-run vitality of the economic and social system. Price level instability is followed closely by the broadly accepted notion that specific social problems require direct action on the part of various governmental units. In his judgment, the public sector's actions often are themselves the source of inflation, and the social problems are frequently made worse by well-meaning intervention.

Though his conclusions are the same, Bolwell's comments are those of a chief executive officer of a firm beset by government regulation, particularly EPA and OSHA. While he believes that "the record of industry in this country is not good enough to justify self-policing in many of these areas," Bolwell's experiences with the various agencies lead him to conclude that their regulations are seldom the best practical way to attain a specific goal, and that often the goals themselves are either conflicting or not worth the cost of attaining them.

Thomas Sowell concludes the first section with an essay that deals with the meaning of two central goals of social policy, poverty and the distribution of income. In it he challenges the implicit presumption of many activists that any improvement in social and economic justice is desirable whatever the costs. In the process, he describes how many apparent problems such as discrimination in employment appear far less serious when the evidence is examined for other variables that may influence the structure of the data, aside from the currently popular categories of race and sex.

The second section contains three articles which address in more detail some of the consequences of interventionist policies. John O'Sullivan's opening essay examines Great Britain as a model of the damage an activist government can do to a society and assesses Mrs. Thatcher's prospects for instituting effective reform. His basic premise is that the civility of Britain's non-competitive egalitarian structure is vanishing under the strain of economic stagnation and the decline in relative affluence of the British people. The traditional explanations for this inferior performance—class structure and loss of empire—are dismissed as incorrect readings of history, and the blame is laid at the feet of interventionist government policy and union activity. In discussing the likelihood of reversing these tendencies, O'Sullivan based his guarded optimism on a public attitude which is more and more antagonistic toward unions, taxes, and government activity. Whether fundamental changes will be forthcoming depends upon whether the public will accept the short-run costs of resource reallocation brought about by policy changes, in exchange for the promise of better times to come.

In the next chapter, Murray L. Weidenbaum provides an overview of the regulatory process in order to provide some insights into the nature of the regulatory costs and why the best of intentions often lead to totally undesirable consequences. His basic conclusion is that blame must be shared by the legislatures for passing laws that create faulty incentive systems, by businesses for resisting efficient policies, and by "public" interest activists whose agendas are at least as narrow as those whose private interests they attack.

The final chapter of Part II is a summary of a study which estimates the costs imposed upon a sample of 48 firms by six federal regulatory bodies: the Environmental Protection Agency, Equal Employment Opportunity, Occupational Safety and Health Administration, Department of Energy, Employee Retirement Income Security Act, and the Federal Trade Commission. Commissioned by The Business Roundtable and carried out by Arthur Andersen & Co., the study attempts to measure the incremental costs borne by business as a result of attempts to comply with the requirements of the six agencies. Included is a summary of methodology as well as an analysis of the incidence of costs by industry.

Part III addresses the issue of finding a solution to the apparent problem of excessive regulation. Thomas A. Murphy, Chairman of General Motors Corporation, opens with a call for reforming federal regulatory practice by eliminating the "one-mission" mentality of individual bureaus and requiring thorough and independent cost-benefit analyses of regulations before they are imposed. In addition, Murphy argues for an end to what he views to be a counterproductive adversary relationship between government and business.

The difficulty of achieving Murphy's goals are all too clearly demonstrated in the following chapter in which Allen R. Ferguson and Murray L. Weidenbaum present their views on the issue of cost–benefit analysis and engage in an informal debate, responding to each other and to questions from the floor. As is often the case, two reasonable authorities on the topic of public policy analysis agree in principle on the appropriate approach to problems but disagree about the value judgments necessary to make the final decision. Nevertheless, if we could accomplish even that much in the national debate on regulation, the cause of rational policymaking would be substantially advanced from its present state.

In the final chapter James F. Gatti addresses the usefulness of various proposals for reform that have been offered under such names as "reindustrialization," "industrial revitalization," or "national planning." There are two basic issues addressed. The first examines the logic of planning in general and its inherent limitations. The second deals with the case of the economic "miracle" of Japan, a frequently cited example of what can be done by government to foster and accelerate economic growth and development.

With respect to the first issue, the conclusion is one of skepticism concerning the potential for government planning in general to provide any net benefits. With respect to the second, a review of the evidence leads him to the conclusion that while the Japanese government created an environment conducive to economic development, little, if any, of the economy's extraordinary growth can be attributed to direct government activity or specific government policies.

The papers do not represent a call for the abolition of the public sector: All of the authors recognize the need for some collectivistic action. Rather, the basic theme is a call for a more objective approach to the selection of the ends and the means of government policies and a thorough evaluation of their consequences. As is the usual case in matters of this sort, an unequivocal conclusion cannot be drawn from the essays, and it is unlikely than an individual holding opposing views will be fully persuaded by the arguments presented in this volume. But that is not its intent. Rather, the goal is to stimulate thought, discussion, and debate on these issues, for it is only through that process that this or any society can hope to develop the broad consensus necessary to select its goals without resort to unacceptable levels of coercion.

CHAPTER 1

An Overview of the Problem of Government Regulation

JAMES F. GATTI

In 1966 George Shultz and Robert Aliber published a book of readings dealing with the efficacy and desirability of wage–price controls in general and the informal and "voluntary" wage–price guidelines in particular. The first section includes an exchange between Milton Friedman and Robert Solow in which they develop the pros and cons of guidelines. Although the topic of their discussion is only tangentially related to the material in this volume, the fundamental error in Solow's position is the same error that has plagued economic policy since the 1930s, and an understanding of that error will provide a useful perspective from which to view this volume.

Friedman begins the discussion with a rejection of any form of formal controls or informal guidelines because, among other things, "voluntary controls invite the use of extra-legal powers to produce compliance. . . . If legal powers granted for other purposes can today be used for the 'good' purpose of holding down prices, tomorrow they can be used for other purposes that will

ISBN 0-12-277620-8 0-12-277622-4(p)

seem equally 'good' to the men in power—such as simply keeping themselves in power."[1]

Solow defends the guidelines as a rather minor intrusion on the freedom of markets and argues: "It is true, I suppose, that Milton may reply that this is after all only the beginning, and great oaks from little acorns grow. Well, as anyone knows who has ever watched a great oak grow from a little acorn, it is not a woosh! It takes a little while."[2]

Had Solow carried the metaphor to its logical long-run conclusion, he might also have observed that the oak, once planted in the garden, ultimately robs the other vegetation of needed sunlight and nutrients! Unfortunately, this failure to consider the long-term consequences is all too characteristic of the process of public policy analysis in much of Western society in general and the United States in particular. Too often warnings of the dangers associated with expanding public sector influence have been dismissed with a variant on Keynes's overused and irrelevant quip,"In the long run, we are all dead."

Although our ultimate mortality as individuals is not a matter of debate, nonetheless two comments on the obsession with the short run are in order. First, it appears that we may well have seriously underestimated our own life expectancies and/or the potential growth rate of government coercion. If not with a "woosh," the oak certainly has grown fast enough to have caused problems within a generation, problems that may well negate any temporary benefits associated with its development. Second, although Keynes can perhaps be excused for taking a short-sighted perspective because he was without progeny, society cannot. If posterity means anything to our society as a whole, we must

[1]Milton Friedman, "What Price Guideposts?" in *Guidelines, Informal Controls, and The Market Place,* eds., George P. Shultz and Robert Z. Aliber (Chicago: University of Chicago Press, 1966), pp. 37–38. Friedman's comments are especially prophetic in light of the actions of the Nixon administration in August, 1971.

[2]Robert M. Solow, "Comments," in Shultz and Aliber, *Guidelines, Informal Controls,* p. 63.

evaluate the implications of policy from a much longer term perspective. This is not to imply that there are no instances in which a greater degree of intervention is desirable. Absolute statements such as that one must be viewed with suspicion. Nevertheless, there is a growing belief, based upon an ever increasing body of evidence, that the long-run effect of a large part of public sector control over private sector activities has been to do, more often than not, more harm than good.

This volume presents the views of some of those individuals who share this belief.

REGULATORY GROWTH

The extraordinary growth of regulation is beyond debate. Ronald J. Penoyer of the Center for the Study of American Business, Washington University, St. Louis, has compiled a volume titled *Directory of Federal Regulatory Agencies*. In it he presents data on the development of agencies as measured by the scope of their powers, employment, budgets, and so on. A simple listing of the agencies and a brief summary of their vital statistics runs to over 100 pages. Figures 1.1 and 1.2 present some of Penoyer's data. As Figure 1.1 clearly shows, the bulk of the growth in the number of agencies is attributable to three decades: that of the Great Depression—the 1930s, and the decades of increased social activism—the 1960s and 1970s. Of the more than 200 years covered, those 30 years account for 70% of all agency growth.

Data on the number of specific pieces of regulatory legislation follow a similar pattern. Thus, in Figure 1.2, which details the decade-by-decade growth of such legislation categorized as to type, the 1930s, 1960s, and 1970s again dominate, contributing 70% of the total legislation.

The parallel in the data is not particularly surprising given the nature of the regulatory process, but the fact that 70% of regulatory activity has taken place in 15% of our history should

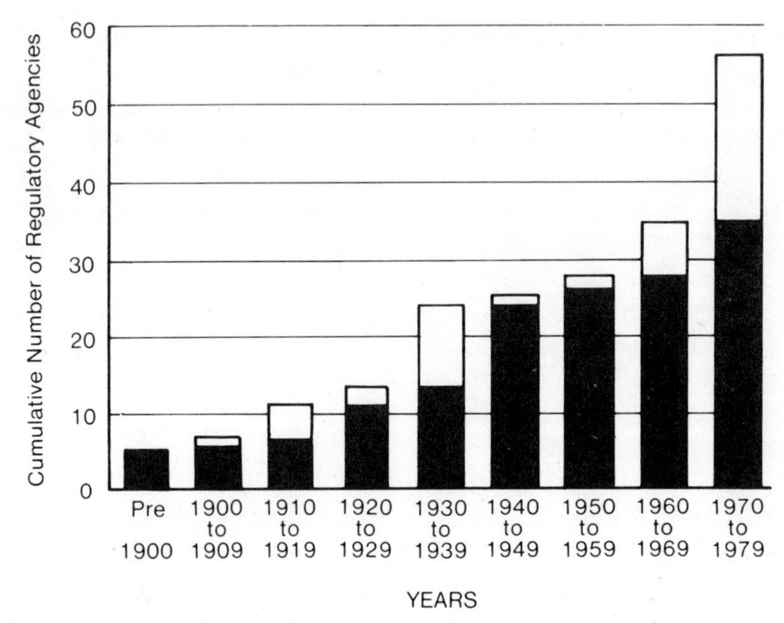

Figure 1.1. A historical perspective to agency growth. (Source: Center for the Study of American Business.)

cause one to pause a bit and consider the implications. Was our society suddenly favored with unique insights concerning the existence of and solutions for a variety of social ills during these two intervals? Or was this simply an emotional and ill-considered response to a set of problems the nature and magnitude of which had never been well established? Again, neither generalization is likely to be an exact description of the situation, but there is a growing feeling that the second is closer to the truth than the first.

The massive and prolonged unemployment and physical deprivation of the 1930s was unprecedented in the short history of capitalist democracy, and the causes of the problem were not generally well understood at the time. The macroeconomic explanation offered by Keynes and the Keynesians was that the free market economic system is inherently unstable, and that acceptable performance could only be obtained via countercyclical tax and spending policies of the central government. The conse-

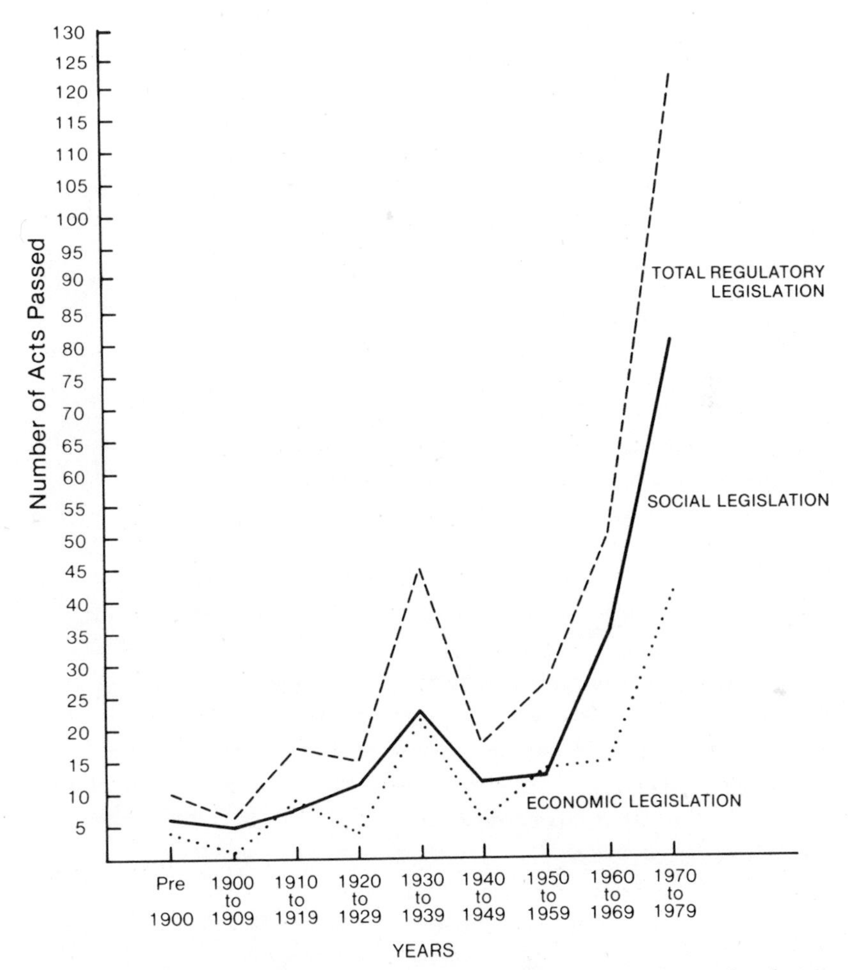

Figure 1.2. A decade-by-decade comparison of major regulatory legislation. (Source: Center for the Study of American Business.)

quences of accepting this economic dogma have been a greater willingness on the part of the central government to incur and tolerate budget deficits, and an almost pathological fear of unemployment however transitory. These have, in turn, been major factors in our accelerating rate of inflation.

The microeconomic corollary to the macro instability has come to be known as market failure, the notion that the concentration of economic power or the lack of "complete" information causes certain groups to be "exploited" and leads markets to perform in undesirable ways. Again, the solution was sought in government action, this time in the form of restricting the ability of individuals to engage in voluntary, and presumably mutually beneficial, transactions. With the exception of financial regulations and laws that increased the power of unions to impose a closed shop, the bulk of the microeconomic restrictions imposed in the 1930s were struck down by the courts as unconstitutional.

Unfortunately, however, the presumption that market failure was the rule rather than the exception did not also die, and it was revived during the activist years of the late 1960s and the 1970s. The stimulus this time was not an economic crisis of the magnitude of that of the 1930s. Instead, it was a popularization of the notion that the problem of pollution and environmental decay was one that, by and large, could not be solved by free market forces. The activism of the environmentalist soon spilled over into other areas of social concern such as workplace safety and consumer protection, and the public sector was called upon to do something about these alleged problems. The result was a veritable explosion of legislation and regulatory bodies whose intent was to correct the perceived ills—whether real or imagined. It is with this set of microeconomic regulations that this volume is most directly concerned.

AN OVERVIEW OF THE REGULATORY CRITIQUE

The general critique of these regulatory policies has three components. The first questions the ability of the public sector to improve the situation; the second questions the choice of policies used; and the third faults policymakers for failing to apply some cost-benefit analysis prior to implementing the specific policies. A good example of the inability of the public sector to improve on the private free market solution can be found in the case of the attempts by the Occupational Safety and Health Administration (OSHA) to insure worker safety by establishing detailed requirements as to design of the workplace. Public policy has failed to bring about a better resolution of workplace safety than the market, because the information needed to structure the solution is far too vast and the individual workplace too varied for centralized control. The information is generally more accessible to the individual worker and firm—and at a far lesser cost—than it is to OSHA. Whether the firm and worker choose to act on that information is another matter and depends upon the incentives to do so. However, in general the private incentive structure is based on the same set of costs and benefits that should be evaluated by OSHA before action is taken. When this sort of situation prevails, it seems best to allow individuals to make decisions that are in their own self-interest, given that they have the same or better information than would be available to the regulators.

The selection of inappropriate policies to attain a specific goal is especially evident in the case of the Environmental Protection Agency (EPA). No one disagrees with the presumption that when environmental damage exists, the external nature of the costs will prevent private decisions from achieving the desired result. However, the EPA's use of arbitrary and uniform standards of permissible effluent and its mandating of specific technologies to solve the problem is clearly counterproductive. It would be far more sensible to levy a charge on the effluent based upon damage done, and allow the firm or individual to determine the appropriate degree of discharge and means to achieve it. If the tax on the next unit of effluent is less than the cost of preventing its discharge, and if the tax is properly set equal to the damage that will be done by that unit, society will be worse off if the reduction is made than if it is not, and the tax is paid by the polluter. This sort of calculus is impossible when standards are arbitrarily set with no regard to incremental costs of pollution.

The failure to apply cost-benefit analyses to the regulatory decision is most dramatic in the case of the Food and Drug Administration (FDA) and the Delaney Amendment, a piece of legislation that absolutely bans proven carcinogens from food products. The goal of reducing the incidence of cancer is noble, but the wording and interpretation of the amendment has been such that bans have been imposed where a significant risk of cancer in laboratory animals exists only when the substance is consumed in absurdly large amounts. Had some sort of cost–benefit standard been applied here and in other areas, the preponderance of the counterproductive regulations would never have been imposed in the first place. Further, in the absence of the patently absurd standards, agency credibility would have been enhanced and beneficial intervention would not have encountered automatic resistance as a result of the stigma attached to other regulation.

CONCLUSION

None of this should be construed to mean that there is no place for public sector interference in what are fundamentally private sector activities. However, it is clear that the ways in which society has attempted to solve very real and pressing problems leaves much to be desired. The chapters that follow attempt to document in more detail the contributors' views as to the nature and the extent of the problem and the possibilities for reform.

PART I

FREEDOM, JUSTICE, AND PUBLIC POLICY

CHAPTER 2

Government Regulation and a Free Society

WILLIAM E. SIMON

Our nation today confronts the persistent problems that have plagued policymakers for more than two decades. All of the claims and promises made over the past two decades are now being tested against the harsh realities of the real world, and the expectations of the people are being matched against the basic capacity of the system to deliver ever more goods and services.

Over the past 20 years the real output of goods and services and the real income of the average American have risen substantially. However, despite these remarkable gains the American people are increasingly dissatisfied with the national state of affairs and their personal status. Part of this frustration is a healthy refusal to tolerate many real problems that exist. The American drive to improve, to help those less fortunate, to seek ever higher personal standards of living is commendable when it leads to a more creative and productive system and increased concern for the needs of others. Unfortunately, the frustration we find in America today also has an unhealthy aspect of cynicism and negativism. I believe that this cynicism and negativism are the result of collec-

ISBN 0-12-277620-8 0-12-277622-4(p)

tivist, big-government approaches to national problems, which promised so much but delivered so little. There has developed a mood of dependence on government, and this mood feeds upon itself, creating still more demands for benefits, without a corresponding recognition that the bills must be paid—either directly in current taxes or indirectly through accelerating inflation and economic disruption.

The elimination of these economic distortions must begin now. The longer we delay the hard adjustment decisions, the more difficult and costly the needed solutions will become. If we delay too long, the opportunities to restore stable economic progress will be lost.

The agenda for America must include an evaluation of the multitude of conflicting claims in order to arrive at the greatest long-term benefit for all of our people. In that process the most important factor to be considered is the freedom and dignity of the individual. Because, no matter what material progress occurs, the loss of personal freedom and dignity is too great a price to be paid. In short, we must decide what kind of economic and political systems will best serve the real long-term interests of the American people while maintaining a free society.

AGENDA FOR THE FUTURE

I will limit myself to a brief review of the basic economic issues that will ultimately shape the future course of the United States. The American people must now decide what kind of economy they want for the foreseeable future. In making that decision, they must realize that their government's fiscal and monetary policies and the maze of government programs that increasingly intervene in their daily lives have an enormous and often adverse impact upon their personal welfare. We must decide

- Whether or not inflation will be effectively controlled or whether it is allowed to remain at double-digit levels

- Whether or not capital investment will be adequate to create meaningful jobs for the growing labor force
- Whether or not government regulation and administrative controls will be changed to meet current economic realities and thus to restore productivity and efficiency
- Whether or not the United States will provide effective leadership on international monetary, trade, and investment issues

In looking to the future, the American people should ask one basic question each time the government comes up with a new economic policy initiative: Will this action contribute to sustained and orderly economic growth or will it merely perpetuate the familiar stop-and-go patterns of the past which have led to the economic and financial disruption caused by chronic deficits, excessive expansion of the money supply, increased government controls over the private economy, and increased intervention in private wage and price decisions?

The proper role of government is to create an environment for sustained and orderly economic growth through fiscal, monetary, and regulatory policies. The disappointing performance of the U.S. economy during much of the last two decades emphasizes the basic need for policies that are more stable. In the mid 1960s the United States began an unfortunate series of exaggerated booms and recessions. Serious overheating of the economy created severe price pressures, and accelerating inflation caused recessions by restricting housing construction, personal spending, and business investment. The recessions created unemployment, which wasted resources and caused personal suffering. This rising unemployment too often triggered poorly planned and ill-timed government fiscal and monetary policies, setting off another round of excessive stimulus leading again to overheating and more government intervention.

Our basic desire for economic progress through improved living standards and employment opportunities will be frustrated unless we better control the insidious inflation which has destroyed economic stability and today threatens not only our goal of sustained growth but the ultimate survival of all of our basic institutions. When inflation distorts the economic system and destroys the incentives for real improvement, the people will no longer support that system and society disintegrates. I am convinced that our uniquely creative and productive society will collapse if we permit inflation to dominate economic affairs. We would be well advised to take heed of an axiom from none other than Lenin himself, who declared that "the best way to destroy the capitalist system is to debase the currency." By a continuing process of inflation, governments can confiscate secretly and unobserved an important part of the wealth of their citizenry, and the sight of this arbitrary rearranging of riches strikes not only at security but also at confidence in the equity of the existing distribution of wealth.

Perhaps we could also learn from a less radical theorist, John Maynard Keynes, who asserted that "There is no subtler, no surer means of overturning the existing basis of society than to debauch the currency. The process engaged all the hidden forces of economic law on the side of destruction and does it in a manner that not one man in a million is able to diagnose."[1]

It is critically important to understand that when I speak of the ills of inflation and recession brought on by an all-powerful government, I am not speaking of narrow economic issues but fundamental issues of equity and social stability. The fact is that throughout history whenever government dominates the economic affairs of its citizens, a free society is eroded, then destroyed, and a minority government ensues. The most important point to be derived is that the free enterprise system and a free society are indivisible. It is impossible to have a politically free society unless the major part of its economic resources is operating under the free enterprise system. The real issue is human freedom (recognizing that the future of the free enterprise system

[1]J. M. Keynes, *The Economic Consequences of the Peace* (New York: Harcourt, Brace & Howe, 1920), p. 236.

is also the future of a free society), and the question we must ask ourselves in analyzing our situation here in America is: Are we going to reverse the trend of the last 40 years toward a collectivist society, or will we choose to ignore history and suffer the inevitable fate of all those countries throughout history, with all the tragic consequences?

The intensity of my feelings about inflation has resulted in some critics labeling me as obsessed. However, I am not so much obsessed as I am downright antagonistic toward those who consistently promote inflationary policies. We must always remember that it is inflation that causes the recessions that so cruelly waste our human and material resources and the tragic unemployment that leaves serious economic and psychological scars long after economic recovery occurs. It is inflation that destroys the purchasing power of our people as they strive, too often in a losing struggle, to provide the necessities of food, housing, clothing, transportation, and medical attention, and to fulfill their need for education, recreation, and cultural opportunities. Inflation is not now, nor has it ever been, the grease that enables the economic machine to progress. Instead, it is the monkey wrench that disrupts the efficient functioning of the system. Inflation should be identified for what it is: the most vicious hoax ever perpetrated for the expedient purposes of a few at the cost of many. There should be no uncertainty about its devastating impact, particularly on low-income families, the elderly dependent on accumulated financial resources, and the majority of working people who do not have the political or economic leverage to beat the system by keeping their incomes rising more rapidly than inflation. There is a kind of quiet hysteria growing in this country, a desperation about how to make ends meet in a time of accelerating costs. In such an atmosphere, people will try anything that offers an illusion of hope, no matter how empty that hope may be.

The tragedy is that the longer inflation continues the worse the consequences will be, not only in economic terms but in political, governmental, and institutional terms as well. It becomes plainer every day that the only alternative to an effective anti-inflation policy is a generalized, undeclared civil war—of taxpayers against government, tenants against landlords, unions against business, farmers against consumers, investors against spenders, and, ultimately, looters against property owners and police.

To avert such catastrophe, there must be more widespread recognition of the fundamental importance of stable economic growth as the only true foundation for maximum employment opportunities and lower unemployment rates. Only a stable real value of the dollar will protect the purchasing power of *all* Americans and encourage the increased capital investment required to provide the permanent and productive jobs that people need. At the same time, this growth must be accompanied by the more efficient use of human and material resources and by the protection of our environment and the fulfillment of our international responsibilities in monetary, trade, and investment policies.

The elimination of inflation need not be at the expense of jobs, for there is no trade-off between the goals of price stability and low unemployment, as some have erroneously claimed. To the contrary, the achievement of the two goals is interdependent. If we are to increase the output of goods and services and reduce unemployment, we must rid our economy of the dreaded disease of inflation. Naturally, there are disagreements about how best to achieve all these basic goals, but I am convinced that a longer term horizon must be used.

First, the diversity of problems must be recognized in order to avoid concentrating on a single issue. Inflation, unemployment, declining output, the availability of productive resources, international trade and investment must all be considered simultaneously to create a balanced program for stable economic growth. The beginning point for sustaining economic growth without the boom and recession distortions of the past is to avoid destructive inflation pressures. From 1890 to 1970, prices in the United States increased at an annual rate of 1.8%. Since then the rate has averaged 6.6%. It seems so obvious that any long-term solution to our economic problems requires better control of inflation which has distorted the spending and savings decisions of all

Americans. Let me repeat that inflation must be clearly recognized for what it is: the greatest threat to the sustained progress of our economy and the personal standard of living of most Americans.

Second, government policies must solve more problems than they create. During a period of difficulty, it is expedient to respond to strident calls "to do something—anything to demonstrate political leadership."

However, this naively activist approach is too often the basic source of problems, not the solution. Courage and wisdom are always required to avoid actions that offer short-term benefits in exchange for further erosion of the free enterprise system. The conventional wisdom that a few billion dollars of additional government spending somehow make the difference between success and failure of the entire U.S. economy (which is rapidly approaching an annual level of output of 2 trillion dollars) has always amazed me. Governments have an important role to play in protecting certain basic public interests, but the claim that governments can or should control the economy is totally false. We would all be better off if government officials would recognize that the real creativity and productivity of America depends on the private sector.

Third, and most important of all, there must be a proper balance in the shared responsibilities of the private and public sectors. This is a difficult assignment because of the confusion and pessimistic appraisals of the future caused by the political and economic shocks that have occurred. Maintaining and improving the creativity and productivity of the U.S. economic system against the attacks of critics who favor a big-government solution for the problems of society have become our greatest challenge. The simplistic cure of having government spend ever increasing amounts of borrowed money has solved few if any of our problems, but it has created serious economic distortions that will continue long into the future. We now have a federal government that is trying to do more than its resources will permit, to do many things that it cannot do very well, and to do some things that it should never do at all. As a result we now have more government than we want, more than we need, and more than we can afford. Nevertheless, much of the current political rhetoric continues to claim that we are not spending enough, are not creating enough new government programs, and are not pushing enough panic buttons. Despite the unmatched accomplishments of the U.S. economy, our critics attack the free enterprise system and demand comprehensive governmental control over economic planning for the allocation of our national resources, the rationing of capital to selected industries, guaranteed government jobs for all who want them, increased control over private economic activities, even a return to the counterproductive wage and price controls that have always failed. Although the American free enterprise system feeds, clothes, and houses people far more effectively than any other system in the world, provides the real basis for all of our public services, and, most importantly, is fundamental to our individual freedoms, it is increasingly subject to criticism. These critics seem to favor turning to less efficient approaches which would waste our human and material resources and eventually erode our economic progress and political freedoms.

Part of the problem is a matter of image. Those who support increased government spending and pervasive controls over our daily lives are often perceived as being more concerned and socially progressive. Those who allegedly "care more" are given considerable attention when they call for more spending to solve the unmet needs of society even though the growth of big government has become a large part of the problem and not the solution it is alleged to be. At the same time, those who favor the free enterprise system too often converse in simplistic slogans that lack humane appeal. Worst of all, many businessmen who come to Washington seem to want to surrender their existing freedoms in exchange for protection from the competition that has made our system so dynamic.

It is now time, indeed the time is long overdue, for those who believe in the free enterprise system to more effectively promote its basic values. America has become the world's premier economy because it provides basic incentives to its people to work hard and to be creative. To the individual family this approach leads to a higher standard of living. To the business firm it means increased markets and larger profits. To our government it means increased effectiveness and public support. Yet, too many Americans, especially those who have known only the affluent society, are unaware of the real source of economic growth in our country. The material abundance, the freedoms of choice, the opportunities for meaningful work are all largely the result of the creativity and productivity of our free and competitive economic system. This is the crucial theme that must be communicated to all Americans until they understand it. The free market economy is the wellspring of our nation's basic strength in every sphere—political, social, military, and economic. It is the source of our present abundance and the basis of our hopes for a better future. We can solve our recognized problems best by preserving and improving and strengthening rather than weakening our uniquely productive system. In doing this we will preserve our other freedoms that have made America so great.

THE CRUCIAL ISSUE IS STILL FREEDOM

The United States now faces—has always faced—a basic choice between private goods and social goals. Yet we hear misleading political rhetoric that we can achieve our basic economic goals without making the necessary sacrifices required to produce and pay for the desired goods and services. Our magnificent country is capable of achieving any of the worthy goals it has identified, but we must face up to many economic realities, particularly the obvious point that goods and services cannot be distributed to the consuming public unless they are first produced. We have the human and material resources necessary to operate our open and competitive economic system and to achieve our goals, if we will create the proper environment. How well we make these basic decisions will ultimately determine what future historians will write about America.

To find the answers we must begin with the correct questions. What has made this a great nation? What has made people throughout the world talk about the American dream? Some argue that it was the good fortune of having the land and natural resources. We have certainly been blessed with an abundance of these resources, but in the Soviet Union we see a land mass that is much larger than our own and equally well endowed. Yet the Soviet system provides much less for its people. They must turn to the United States for the grain they need to feed them and for our technology and capital.

Does our strength depend only on the qualities of our people? We are clearly blessed with one of the largest and most talented populations that the world has ever known. However, in China today we see a population that is four times as large as our own, whose civilization at one time was developed far in advance of the rest of the world. Yet their present material standard of living and personal freedoms are most disappointing.

Thus, although our land, resources, and people have been essential parts of the American story, there is a third factor that has contributed to America's progress, a factor that is too often missing in other countries. That crucial factor has been our national commitment to liberty and individual dignity. For 200 years people have streamed to our shores in search of various freedoms—freedom of religion, freedom of speech, freedom of the press, freedom of assembly, and freedom to seek their fortunes without fear or favor of the government. All of these freedoms are planted firmly in our constitution. But they have become such a familiar part of our lives that I wonder whether we now take them too much for granted. There is nothing artificial about freedom, nor is there any guarantee of its permanency. As Dwight Eisenhower once said, "Freedom has its life in the hearts, the actions, and the spirits of men, and so it must be daily earned and refreshed—else, like a flower cut from its life-giving roots, it will wither and die."

There are many ways this can happen, some of them very slow and subtle. For example, there has been an accelerating trend toward collectivist policies in the United States as people have been persuaded that the problems of our society have become so large that individuals can no longer cope with them. Many Americans now expect the government to assume responsibility for solving their problems and to do things for them that they once did for themselves. Government has been gradually cast in the role of trying to solve all the difficult challenges of modern life.

That trend began to accelerate in the 1960s as governments promised the rapid solution of complex political, economic, and social problems and an end to economic cycles through the clever manipulation of government policies. We failed to note that resources are always limited, even in a nation as affluent as ours. Unfortunately, the inflated expectations and broken promises of the past have left a residue of disillusionment. Many young people are skeptical about our basic institutions, and I cannot say that I blame them. International problems, the energy crisis, disappointing harvests, excessive government regulations, wage and price controls, and thousands of other specific problems have contributed significantly to the high levels of inflation and unemployment. But the underlying momentum has been basically caused by the excessive economic stimulus provided by the federal government for more than two decades. We experienced a quintupling of the federal budget in just 15 years, a string of 19 budget deficits in 20 years, and a tripling of the national debt in just 15 years time.

The greatest irony of these misguided policies is that they were based on the mistaken notion that they would specifically help the poor, the elderly, the sick, and the disadvantaged. Yet when these stop-and-go government policies trigger inflation and unemployment, who gets hurt the most?—the very same people the politicians claimed they were trying to help: the poor, the elderly, the sick, and the disadvantaged.

Even more fundamentally, the last 15 years have seen an acceleration of the trend toward big government and the diminishing of economic and personal freedoms in the United States. The federal government has now become the dominant force in our society. It is the biggest single employer, the biggest consumer, and the biggest borrower. Fifty years ago, its spending comprised approximately 10% of the gross national product, today that figure exceeds 35%. If the federal government spending trends of the last two decades continue, its share of economic activity in the United States will be approaching 60% by the year 2000. As the government exercises more and more influence in the economy, its control of the personal decisions of its citizenry will increase proportionally. History shows that when economic freedom disappears, personal and political freedoms also disappear. The inextricable relationship between economic freedom and personal freedom is sometimes overlooked by those who constantly seek to expand the powers of government, but it is plain to see in many countries around the world where these freedoms have been lost.

Unfortunately, there is no convenient scapegoat on which to blame our problems. As modern governments have usurped the power to increasingly control our daily lives, they have done so with good intent, thinking that they are the proper authority to determine and then implement the ideals of society. In other words, governments have sacrificed individual freedoms for a collective system of rules that served to impose their view of what is best for each of us, yet this behavior has been merely a reflection of what governments believed the people wanted. Thus it is not "the government" that we should blame. That is a simplistic excuse. The blame belongs to the institutions of society, including the colleges and universities, which have created an environment in which equality of status is mistaken for equality of opportunity, and security is exchanged for personal freedom. The result has been, as mentioned earlier, an increasing mood of frustration and skepticism about our ability to handle the problems of the future. If this trend continues, most of the freedoms that we cherish will not survive, for personal, political, and economic freedoms are all intertwined and cannot exist alone. The great historian Edward Gibbon is said to have made this observation in an evaluation of ancient Greece:

> In the end, more than they wanted freedom, they wanted security. They wanted a comfortable life and they lost it all—security, comfort, and freedom. When the Athenians finally wanted not to give to society, but for society to give to them, when the freedom they wished for most was freedom from responsibility, then Athens ceased to be free.

Our basic challenge, then, is to determine how much personal freedom, if any, we are willing to give up in seeking the false security of a collectivist society. It is certainly not easy to live with the uncertainties that exist in a free society, but the real personal benefits created render the system far superior to any other system. It is this heritage of personal freedom that has made America a land blessed above all others. To protect this remarkable privilege is a goal worthy of our greatest personal and institutional commitment. If we fail in this regard, then the irrational, unrealistic fiscal, monetary, tax, and regulatory policies of nearly half a century will have so damaged our economy that financial collapse will be probable within this century.

If the collapse does occur, the United States will, in my judgment, simultaneously turn into an economic dictatorship. So many citizens have been trained to see the government as economically omniscient and omnipotent, and to blame all economic ills on "business," that disaster could easily bring popular demand for a takeover of the major means of production by the state. Legal precedent and ideological justification exist. It would take little to accomplish the transition.

In summary, the agenda calls for political courage and public wisdom—our only hope for preserving the premier economy of the world as well as our individual freedoms. We must make all Americans aware of the fact that the fundamental guiding principles of American life have been reversed, and that we are careening with frightening speed toward socialism and away from individual sovereignty, toward coercive centralized planning and away from free individual choice. We must generate broad-based support for a plan to reduce the growth of federal spending, match the growth of the money supply to the true growth of the economy, reduce taxes, and eliminate unnecessary regulation.

The longer we delay the hard decisions, the less likely we are to succeed. The American people must now decide whether they will sell the liberty that is the envy of the world for the empty promise of the welfare state, or whether they will restrict government to its proper functions: defense of the nation, protection of the helpless, and creation of an environment for sustained economic growth through sensible fiscal, monetary, tax, and regulatory policies.

We must never forget that personal and political freedoms are inseparable from economic freedom. Tell those who characterize the fight for liberty as "reactionary" that, in the context of history, coercion is clearly reactionary and liberty progressive. Tell them that the twin ideas of human liberty and the free market were born only yesterday. Tell them that allowing millions upon millions of individuals to pursue their material interests, with minimal interference from the state, will unleash an incredible and orderly outpouring of inventiveness and wealth. Tell them that lack of vision threatens to extinguish the brightest light ever to appear in the history of the human race. Tell them about America.

CHAPTER 3

A New Threat to Freedom: The Challenge of the 1980s

HARRY J. BOLWELL

At the start of every decade, there is a great temptation for speakers to try to gaze into the fog of the future and predict some of the key events of the next 10 years. In preparing my remarks for today, I looked at some speeches made at the beginning of the 1970s, and was somewhat startled to discover how wrong many predictors were. There were many rosy forecasts about the technological marvels that would occur during the 1970s; how Americans would benefit materially from the new age; and how we were likely to end the decade richer and happier than ever before.

In short, as we entered the 1970s, America's mood was optimistic. Domestic oil was still filling about 75% of our total annual consumption. Gasoline and other petroleum products were inexpensive and plentiful. Virtually no one foresaw the energy crisis that burst upon us just 3 short years later. It was not foreseen that by the end of the decade we would be dependent on foreign sources for nearly 50% of our oil, which would be both scarce and expensive. And virtually none of the predictors envi-

ISBN 0-12-277620-8 0-12-277622-4(p)

sioned the mood of pessimism that prevails today as we attempt to deal with double-digit inflation, lofty interest rates, deteriorating relations with other countries, and a host of other problems.

You can quickly conclude from this that I decided not to try to predict the future for you today. But I do want to set you to thinking about some of the things that should and should not happen during the 1980s.

Several years ago at a graduation ceremony at Harvard, George Plimpton, with tongue in cheek, suggested that students not go out into the world—there was no room for them. I must emphatically disagree with this advice. My advice to you is just the opposite. I say, come out into the world. We need your skills and vitality. We need your involvement—not only in the business world, but in community and political activities as well. There is a lot of work to be done. The simple fact is that the university is no longer a sanctuary from the problems of the real world—if it ever was. Universities today face the same problems as are faced by those of us in business and other segments of society.

In a newly published book containing a number of essays on the outlook for the United States during the 1980s, John H. Bunzel, former president of San Jose State University and now a senior research fellow at Stanford's Hoover Institute, sounded like many of today's businessmen when he described one problem of the modern university. He said, and I quote:

> Campuses see their autonomy slipping away as the result of increasing federal intervention, through what academics regard . . . as power-wielding bureaucrats bent on enforcing a particular principle or law. . . . The academic community is virtually of one mind in opposing the transfer of more and more authority and decision-making from educational institutions to government officials.[1]

The politicizing of the classroom is a real issue today, and one that

[1]John H. Bunzel, "Higher Education: Problems and Prospects," "The United States in the 1980s," Peter Duignan and Alvin Rabushka, Hoover Institute Publication 220, Palo Alto, California, 1980, p. 408.

I agree deserves stiff resistance on the part of academics. But this is only one symptom of what might accurately be termed "our over-regulated era." I suggest that one of the crucial problems facing this nation during the 1980s is how we go about stemming the alarming growth of control over all of our lives.

Many of you will be entering the business world after graduation. When you do, you will undoubtedly be amazed at the degree of regulation, on every level, you will encounter. At my own company, we are currently spending some $55 million to expand our foundries to keep up with the demand for freight cars. But some 20% of this represents the cost of meeting regulations that did not even exist a few years ago.

The Center for the Study of American Business has estimated that the cost of complying with government regulations was $103 billion for 1979 alone. A recent steel industry study estimates that the engineering control changes to meet noise standards set by the Occupational Safety and Health Administration (OSHA) would cost $1.2 million for each affected worker. The steel industry claims that it can provide better protection for only $42 per employee, by the way.

This case is not too surprising when you consider another case a few years ago, in which the Department of Labor issued a regulation wherein lift trucks in factories had to be equipped with horns to warn workers when the trucks came close to them. Six months later, OSHA issued its own regulations requiring that employees use earmuffs to protect them from the noise of the horns.

In yet another case, one of our foundries was required to replace traditional wet scrubbers for cleaning sand used in making molds for steel castings with dry scrubbers because someone decided the phenols used in the wet process might be harmful if released into the atmosphere. We have since learned that ordinary maple trees release more phenols into the air annually than our scrubbing process ever could. Maple trees, maple syrup—think about that for a moment.

I mention these examples not to imply that business and industry do not need to be regulated, but to give you an idea of the many, and often conflicting, rules and regulations that beset us today.

I am sure you would object if I, or anyone else, claimed that environmental protection laws ought to be thrown out, or that the Occupational Safety and Health Administration and numerous other agencies should be abolished. The record of industry in this country is not good enough to justify self-policing in many of these areas. Our lakes and streams did not get polluted by themselves. And the air around our cities did not get filled with sulfur dioxide and other pollutants without a lot of help from industry. (Of course, automobiles, municipal sewer discharges, and the like also contributed.) In short, we must have laws and regulations to protect us. But must this be accomplished by rigid control over every aspect of our lives?

Thomas Jefferson, in his inaugural address, described the type of government he had helped to create and which he fervently hoped would continue. He called it "a wise and frugal government which shall restrain men from injuring one another, shall leave them otherwise free to regulate their own pursuits of industry and improvement, and shall not take from the mouth of labor the bread it has earned."

I am certain Jefferson never envisioned the rapid growth of government as it has evolved over the last several years. The number of federal employees alone now numbers some 3 million people. And they are making decisions that affect the daily lives and freedom of choice of every one of us—and, I might add, take quite a bit of "bread" we have earned by our labor.

This control and encroachment of freedom takes place not just against business and industry, although business is a target that is being zeroed in on at the moment. That is a subject I will get into a bit later. Regulation and control are also affecting every other major segment of society—universities, hospitals, the professions. I will cite two examples in fields with which I have recently become familiar—medical education and hospitals.

Two years ago, the government established a regulation

whereby medical schools were forced to admit a certain number of third-year students who had previously attended medical schools in foreign countries. This requirement took no cognizance of the educational qualifications of the students from foreign schools. The government said that any medical school that failed to comply with the requirement would lose the federal funds it had been receiving. In this particular case, several medical schools announced they would nonetheless refuse to participate. This required courage on the part of the faculties of the medical schools. The loss of federal funds meant that many worthwhile programs would have to be cut back. Despite this, the faculties did make this decision. When the agencies in Washington heard of this, they reacted. The reaction was even more vindictive: Unless the faculties changed their position, cut-offs would involve not only federal funds, but also federal loans to needy students. When this threat was made public, certain members of Congress told the agencies to "back off." However, proposals are still being debated that will impose curriculum and other requirements upon medical schools.

In hospitals, too, we see the heavy hand of control. Laws are often enacted by Congress for one purpose, only to have that purpose subverted by bureaucrats who make up regulations that provide a different interpretation of the original law. A case in point was a section of the Social Security amendments of 1972 that denied Medicare and Medicaid reimbursement to hospitals for costs "that flow from marked inefficiency in operations or conditions of excessive service."

At University Hospital in Cleveland, there is an excellent 20-bed intensive care unit, which is divided into a 10-bed critical section and a 10-bed progressive section, where patients are taken when they need slightly less monitoring and personal observation. Clearly this is not inefficient or excessive service, but it does cost more than an ordinary hospital room. Two years ago, Medicare auditors cited the Social Security amendments clause in denying hospital reimbursement for intensive care costs at both sections, cutting the per bed allowance in half. The position was that the intensive care section was not intensive as it was connected to the progressive care section, which was not intensive because it allowed some privacy and family visitations. The decision by the government department caused us to close eight beds in this unit. Keep in mind that University Hospital is a hospital that admits any and all patients. It is located in the heart of urban Cleveland. The intensive care unit has saved lives—the closing of these beds cost lives. We finally won a reversal of this ruling, after spending thousands of dollars in attorney fees and countless hours of staff time.

Fortunately, people are beginning to balk at such "Catch 22" decision making. There is a great danger when political objectives are tied to funding or regulation-making. Such actions take away freedom from all of us. Freedom is not divisable. You cannot deny basic rights to one segment of the society, without denying them to every segment, right down to the individual. And I submit, it is our basic birthright of freedom that is at stake as we enter the 1980s. There is a real danger that the state will take over our lives unless individuals—you and I—react and do our best to help stem the tide.

In this vein, I should comment on the Big Business Day activities set for tomorrow around the country. I am sure you know what I am referring to: a series of events that have been organized by Ralph Nader and others as an attempt to gain support for a piece of legislation they have titled "the Corporate Democracy Act of 1980." I do not see how anyone who knows anything about the operations of business in this country can agree with this designation. The so-called Corporate Democracy Act would not bring about corporate democracy at all. Instead it would impose still greater control over the corporation than already exists. And the corporation is already the most regulated institution in American society. I will not go into great detail on the proposals. You will see and hear enough of that in your newspapers and on television tomorrow.

In a recent article, Herbert Stein called the proposed legislation the beginning of "a decade-long attempt to brainwash the American people into thinking that the large corporation, which is the most visible manifestation of the free enterprise system, is the enemy of the people."[2] He said the most serious results would be, not passage of the act, which is only the incidental vehicle of the movement, but the ever greater willingness to tax and regulate the corporation, greater reluctance of savers to invest in them, and weakened morale of their managers. I, too, perceive the real crux of the problem as lying, not in the specific proposals contained in the proposed legislation, but in the total effect. I agree completely with Herbert Stein and others who believe that the main purpose of Big Business Day—or more correctly, Anti-Business Day—is to discredit the American corporation. It takes only a casual reading of the provisions of the proposal and of statements by Ralph Nader and others to determine that these proposals would completely change the structure of the corporation and destroy the very fabric of a system that has made America the most productive society the world has ever known.

I will just mention one part of the proposed legislation, and that is a proposal whereby a corporation could not move a plant without lengthy public hearings. This is to say that a plant could not be moved from Ohio to Texas, or, for instance, Vermont. Does this mean the people of Texas or Vermont cannot be offered the opportunity to work for $15 an hour as do the workers in Ohio? And if this legislation is passed, what is next? Let us assume you are an engineer or an accountant and doing very valuable work at a plant in Ohio. Can it be that you will be prevented from taking a position in Texas or Vermont because you are needed for the economy of that town in Ohio? Believe it or not, we do not move plants in order to pay a lower wage at a different location. We move them because of factors such as obsolescence, availability of work force, and productivity of the work force.

I would like to suggest that there is a great hypocrisy behind this movement. It is coming at a time when America feels beset by problems, and these professional protesters have seized upon the basic feeling of uncertainty to identify business as the scapegoat.

[2]Herbert Stein, "Let's Hold a 'No-Business Day,'" *The Wall Street Journal*, January 7, 1980.

This is the problem. The real issues are dismissed. Media events are created and the serious issues are reduced to a single slogan. The demagogue pointing to a scapegoat is not new. The leadership of Germany in the 1930s found a scapegoat and used that scapegoat as the cause of all the economic problems in that country. Business may contribute to our problems, but business is not the sole cause of our problems any more than is the medical profession, academia, or the legal profession.

It is comforting to have a scapegoat. If we do, we do not have to blame ourselves; if we do, we do not have to be part of the problem. This, then, is hypocrisy, as each one of us is part of the problem.

What the American people have to face is that the problems are real and will not be solved by sloganeering. There is an energy shortage. Big business did not cause the shortage. It has come about because we have been using more oil than we produce and we use it in the wrong places. There is no reason in the world why oil should be used to generate electricity, as it has been here in the East. There is no reason why Americans should continue to drive their cars with gasoline kept at an artificially low price that is less than half what drivers in other countries have been paying. A few years ago in Portugal, I noticed that during rush hour, many workers flooded the roadways with little motor scooters. I will bet that not many of them would have turned down a chance to drive to work in a large American car. But gasoline at that time was more than $2 a gallon in Portugal, and they could not afford the luxury.

We will not solve our problems by debating about corporate governance laws, or by trying to pin blame on who got us where we are in the first place. The fact is that we are going to have to pay the world price for petroleum, and we are going to have to create solutions to energy shortages and other problems.

In my opinion, what we need is, first, the honesty as a people to face these problems; and, second, the courage to solve them. The problems of the world will not be solved by people afraid to back up their convictions with action. If I can leave you with one thought today, it is this: If there are two qualities that we need most, they are integrity and courage. The kind of courage I am talking about is the courage that does not hide behind slogans or easy solutions. Look at the facts, perceive the problem, and go about solving it in the best way you can. The voice of the demogogue should have no place in deciding your future. If you can augment what you have learned here with that sense of personal integrity, the courage and the will to shape your own destiny, then we can breathe easier. The freedom we all cherish is in jeopardy. But that is nothing new. It always has been. It is up to you and me—and every American—to work at keeping it.

CHAPTER 4

Poverty, the Distribution of Income, and Social Policy: Some Thoughts

THOMAS SOWELL

This chapter is a collection of thoughts on poverty, the distribution of income, and social policy. The topic is a highly emotional one, and discussions of it are often complicated by a misunderstanding of the concepts involved. If I may, I would like to begin by making some distinctions among them.

POVERTY VERSUS THE DISTRIBUTION OF INCOME

When the public is concerned about the alleviation of poverty, they are anxious that children should not go to bed hungry, that families should not live in leaky, rat-infested homes. They are saying that there is some minimum standard of material living that should be enjoyed by all members of the society. The precise level of that standard can be and is debated, but the general goal is quite clear.

The term *income distribution* on the other hand is really a misnomer. Most income—whether in Communist, capitalist, or

ISBN 0-12-277620-8 0-12-277622-4(p)

any other kind of society—is *earned*, not distributed. It represents payment for services rendered personally or by one's property in the case of private property societies. By contrast, newspapers are distributed. They are produced at one place and distributed to points of sale. But income from the production of newspapers is earned, and those earnings are proportional to the value placed on the output by the purchasers.

As a practical matter, it is poverty, not the distribution of income, that concerns the public. Adequate food, clothing, and shelter—however defined—are the goal. The public does not care whether plumbers earn more income than dentists or dentists more than plumbers. They do not care whether the middle 20% of income earners receive more or less than 20% of the national income. Even the poor are unconcerned about redistribution to equalize income. Polls among blacks, for example, find that more than four times as many blacks believe that income should vary according to individual productivity as believe in even approximate equality—much less the kind of equality proposed by social reformers.

Problems arise because some individuals—typically intellectuals, politicians, and journalists—are concerned with eliminating what they call "disparities" or "inequities" in the distribution of income, wealth, or economic power. Politically, this group of redistributionists promotes its goals by playing on the public's concern over poverty and its alleviation. Most of the schemes that involve transfer payments to redistribute income have been sold to the public as a solution to concrete deprivation. Many of these programs began in the Great Depression, when such deprivations were general throughout society. In later periods, the poverty of *specific* groups—"minorities," the aged, and residents of depressed regions—served as the rationale for various schemes of *general* redistribution.

General redistribution has also been promoted by attacking the justification for the existing pattern of income payments. However, one must recognize that income distribution is simply a set of retrospective statistics. As such, it represents earlier interactions among individual capabilities, ownership of physical capital, preferences for occupations, and the demand for various outputs of goods and services. Payments that have been made for these outputs have been justified by the individual purchasers. The grand totals have not been justified by anyone. It is not at all clear that some third party exists who has the omniscience needed to pass judgment on that pattern.

REWARDS BASED ON STATUS VERSUS BEHAVIOR

If the prevailing distribution is to be replaced, one must offer some other basis for rewards than the demand for one's output. There is a tendency among redistributionists to attempt to base rewards—indeed, to base decisions in general—upon status rather than behavior. In the specific case of income distribution, it is argued that the recipients of these various transfers have a status, an equal status, which should determine their income. That is, they have an equal status as a citizen, or as a human being that requires income to be either a so-called "decent minimum" or some amount ranging all the way up to an equal share of national income. The specific level depends upon where the advocate is on the political spectrum.

This line of argument puts great emphasis on the concern with an *equal* status. The more fundamental question is whether decisions ought to be based upon *any* status rather than on assessments of behavior. That is, the question is not whether there shall be equality of status, but whether any status-based decision should supercede decisions based on behavior.

One of the differences between rewarding people for their status rather than their behavior is that the decisions have to be made by entirely different groups of people. If you are rewarding people for their behavior, then those people who acquire the services performed will decide individually—millions of them—whether those services are worth what is being asked for them. But if decisions are based on status (and it does not matter for this purpose whether that status is equality, superiority, or inferiority), then some small group of people must decide what that status is and they must then confer that status on, or deny it to, millions of other human beings. This involves the concentration of substantial political power, regardless of whether the decision concerns the income to be received or admission to a university.

The concentration of power occurs regardless of the degree of public support for the particular status relationship. For instance, consider a society in which racism is very widespread, such as the Republic of South Africa today or the South in nineteenth-century America. In these societies there is (was) a solid consensus that race should play a major role in all decisions—salary, criminal punishment, ability to travel, voting, occupation, etc. Yet even with this consensus, the white population with the power enjoyed markedly less personal freedom than contemporaries in less racist societies. It is not coincidental that the whites in South Africa today are less free than the white population in most of the countries of Western Europe. It is impossible to carry out status-based decisions without superceding the judgments of the individual, and if you do that, you reduce the individual's freedom.

One could write a very large book on all the mechanisms required in the South to maintain the racial system that existed, even though there was a broad consensus among the white citizens about that system. That was true even under slavery. There were generally accepted notions about how slaves ought to be treated. Yet because various individuals were profit maximizers and sometimes found these notions in conflict with their best interests, they continually violated the rules. As a result, the government was continually passing laws in the South, particularly in the cities, which prescribed the proper treatment of slaves—usually condemning the leniency of some profit-maximizing slave owners. One of the fascinating things about the laws in the antebellum Southern cities was how often the same law got passed over and over again in the same city. This suggests that the original law was violated so pervasively that people were not even aware that it was on the books. As a result, legislators passed it again and again in the hope of forcing the individual to base his decisions on status rather than behavior.

Given the diversity of human beings and the diversity of their performances, and given the diversity of other human beings' perceptions of performance, there is *no* status that can be universally and voluntarily accepted in *any* form of society. To say that you are for status-based decisions is to say that you are in favor of forcibly imposing a given status from the top down.

The whole distinction between status and behavior goes beyond questions of income distribution. For example, there are many rights created for various groups which require that individuals assigned to that group be treated according to the status that is ascribed to them collectively, rather than according to the individual behavior which people observe. This began with groups which were defined by biological characteristics—race, sex, etc. But, over time, this was extended to groups defined by their *behavior*—for example, criminals, homosexuals, alcoholics, addicts. Various laws have been passed prohibiting discrimination against these people on these bases. In other words, they are to be treated according to some central group's notion of what their status ought to be rather than according to the behavioral assessments of employers or other people who might transact or interact with them.

In the case of sex, differentiation has been fought on status grounds even where there are demonstrable differences in behavior. For example, the courts have restricted the ability of employers to provide different pension fund benefits or require different payments to the funds, despite the demonstrable fact that women live longer than men. A woman's life expectancy is 78 years, compared to 70 for a man, which means that the postretirement period for women is more than double that for men. One would normally expect that to be reflected in the pension fund benefits (given equal payments), or in the pension fund payments (for the same benefit level). The law says that cannot happen, because it would be a violation of equal status. The logic of that, if you carried it far enough, is that we would ultimately end up with homes for unwed fathers, because their status would clearly be the same as that of unwed mothers, though their behavior is radically different.

Even when we turn to decisions based on behavior, conflicts can arise. Behavior can be assessed either by results or by some estimate of effort. Very often, you hear the argument that this group or that group is losing out, that they deserve better. For example, the argument has been made recently that the Chrysler Corporation is now in deep financial trouble through no fault of its own. Of course people who are heartless, like economists, would argue "Who *cares* whether it was any fault of their own?"

If you are going to judge fault and merit, then you risk freezing the existing set of conditions, whatever they may happen to be. If you are going to reallocate resources as the society's tastes or technology changes, or as new methods of organization become possible, then at some stage you are going to have to move people out of where they are into new places where they are more productive. And the way that that is done is by paying less to people who do the exact same amount of work, take the same risks, and have the same diligence. All the Boy Scout virtues may be the same between two groups, and yet one group will find itself earning much less in a given occupation or sector of the economy. That, of course, is the very reason why they leave that occupation or sector. If you are going to reward them for merit, you will give them absolutely no incentive to move out of obsolete industries and into industries producing new products with higher demand.

Even individual output is not an unambiguous measure of "worth." The number of home runs hit by Babe Ruth was not purely a matter of his individual performance. If you look at his record, you will find that in some years before he hit the 60 home runs he had higher batting averages, higher slugging averages, and hit home runs with greater frequency than he did in 1927. Why then did he hit the 60 home runs in 1927? Because batting after him in 1927 was a young man named Lou Gehrig, who batted .373 with 47 home runs and 175 runs batted in. The situation facing the pitcher was either to pitch to Ruth with x number of men on base or to Gehrig with $x + 1$ men on base. Many pitchers decided they would just as soon pitch to Ruth. In fact, when you find sluggers who run up very high totals of home runs—Ruth, Aaron, Maris—they always did so batting ahead of someone else who was just about equally dangerous as a hitter. Aaron batted ahead of Eddie Mathews (who once hit 47 home runs, for those for whom Eddie Mathews is ancient history). Roger Maris received very few bases on balls the year he hit 61 home runs. He was batting ahead of Mickey Mantle, who hit home runs with greater frequency, but who just did not have as many times at bat. There was absolutely nothing to be gained by walking Maris to pitch to Mantle.

Thus, even in things that are individual in nature, performances are conditioned by a whole set of circumstances over which the individual has no control. One of the sad things that has happened is that both the political left and the political right have seized on the notion of merit as either justifying income or as what ought to justify income. On the right, you find people like John Bates Clark, who developed marginal productivity theory, arguing that because people were paid their marginal product, therefore they were being rewarded for their merit. But of course, their marginal products depended upon all the other cooperating factors with which they were working. It depended upon the way they themselves were raised, upon the whole capital of the country in which they happen to have been born. Had you been born 100 years earlier or in some other part of the world, your income could be half or a tenth of what it is right now, independent of your personal merit. On the left, of course, you have the utopian "to each according to his needs." The state of Soviet agriculture is mute testimony to the bankruptcy of that approach.

POVERTY: ITS MEANING AND MEASUREMENT

None of this, of course, is to assert that poverty does not exist as a problem with which society should be concerned. Poverty and the distribution of income are distinct concepts. However, there are problems with the different meanings of poverty. A basic conception of poverty is the existence of people who are below some given living standard over some substantial period of time. You might argue whether the standard should be cash income only or whether in-kind transfers should be included. You might also modify this by raising the question of whether poverty should be looked at retrospectively or prospectively. Retrospectively, we can consider how much income someone earned over a given period. And yet, people may have very good prospects and choose not to exercise them. One can be a beach bum with a graduate degree, as is, in fact, not all that uncommon in California. Shall we say that the beach bum is poor because—looking back over some period of time—his income was low? His income might be lower than that of, say, an unskilled factory worker. Would we say that he is poorer than the factory worker in any meaningful sense of the word, when at any given time he may exercise his options and earn a greater income?

The question is not what is the right and proper definition of poverty. The more fundamental point is that whatever meaning we give to poverty, that meaning is frozen into statistics; it is also frozen into our laws governing the benefits due the poor. That is what poverty means, once we have committed ourselves to a legal definition, regardless of how ludicrous the results after the fact. We should distinguish the poor as we conceive of them from the poor as they appear in our statistics and in our laws. With a sufficiently narrow definition of income, the statistical "poor" might include, for example, a Kennedy or a Rockefeller who happened not to be working this year. One of the advantages of having wealth is that you do not have to work, or work as hard, or seek out jobs that pay you the highest income. You can pick jobs that would give you the most pleasure, or the most visibility (for political or other purposes). In no sense of the word are you poor just because your income is low. People who graduate by the millions each June only earn half as much that year as they would normally earn. Therefore, their income may fall into the poverty level, even though they are not poor in any meaningful sense.

A more fundamental problem is that people typically, over

their lifetimes, earn different amounts of income at different stages. When they start out they usually earn very little, because they have very little to offer an employer. As they acquire more skills and experience, as employers know more about them, and workers know more about how to look for and perform on a job, then of course their incomes tend to rise. Statistical "income distribution" data freeze all these people at different phases of their life cycles at one moment. We talk about the bottom quarter as if they were the poor in the sense in which we conceive of the poor as being people who over some substantial period of time lack a certain standard of living. The big problem is keeping clear the distinctions between our conceptions and what is in those statistics.

Age bracket differences are very substantial. They are greater than black–white differences in income. Families headed by people in their mid forties to mid fifties earn income in excess of the income of the family headed by someone 25 and under by a greater amount than white incomes exceed black incomes. Two-thirds of all the top wealth holders of the nation are over 50 years of age. We conceive of this top 1% or 5% of wealth holders as the Gettys, Hunts, and Rockefellers. They are much more likely to be some elderly home owner who has finally paid off his mortgage. Outright ownership of the average home would be sufficient to put you in the top 1–2% of wealth holders in the United States. The Hunts and Rockefellers are indeed in there, but they are an insignificant part of the total. The very same person, of course, can be in different quartiles of the income distribution in different parts of his life. This person who pays off his mortgage when he is over 50 may be in the top quarter of income earners then even though he was in the bottom quarter when he was 20. It is very different to be concerned about the fact that there are people who are poor throughout their lifetimes than to be concerned over the fact that young people do not yet earn as much as their parents or their grandparents. If you are thinking about setting up programs to help the poor as defined by the bottom $x\%$ of the income distribution, think again. You really do not need a federal program to help young people become parents and grandparents. They have been doing it for quite some time, without any help from Washington.

THE SOURCE OF POVERTY

To say that gross statistical measures of poverty overstate the problem does not, of course, mean that the problem is not worthy of our attention. Yet I have a lot of difficulty with the notion of the "causes" of poverty. Poverty is simply the absence of wealth. If you look at the history of the world, you find that poverty has been prevalent through most of that history. Even countries that are now rich were once poor, and typically not that far back in history. Yet the discussion goes on as if there were some predestined prosperity that is somehow thwarted by some intervening factor which we must discover.

At this point it is useful to distinguish between moral explanations and causal explanations. There is no a priori reason why something that is a very important moral factor has to be an important causal factor, or vice versa. Nevertheless, this is a recurrent presumption in many studies and conclusions. There are many morally very important factors—slavery or discrimination, for example—which many people presume are important causally in explaining poverty and various other kinds of intergroup differences today. Conversely, there are many other important causal factors which have no moral content, and which are ignored. As noted previously in the case of wealth, age is a major factor in explaining intergroup differences, yet most people are unaware of the degree to which groups differ in age. The average age of Jews in the United States is 46, the average of Polish-Americans 40, Irish-Americans 36, Japanese-Americans 32, Chinese 28, blacks 22, Mexican-Americans 18, Puerto Ricans 18. These are not negligible differences. These differences run into the decades, and even to more than a quarter of a century from one group to another. So when numbers are tossed around about how this group is $x\%$ of the population but earns only $y\%$ of the income, you are talking about groups that differ by decades in their age alone, quite aside from other kinds of differences that are very important.

In the area of race, there are many heavily moral factors that are assumed to be heavily important causal explanations of poverty. Yet very little effort has been made to actually test whether that is so or not. For instance, in the United States there are not only the native black Americans, there are also black Americans of West Indian ancestry who have come here and who, certainly after a generation or so, are virtually indistinguishable by most whites or, for that matter, by most blacks. But, although blacks in general have an income that is only 62% of that of whites, West Indian blacks living in the United States have an income that is 94% of that of whites.

Even when this is perceived and accepted, some people have argued that it is because there has been a difference in treatment. We can test that argument by examining second generation West Indians. If white employers, for example, are distinguishing between two groups of blacks by accent, by birthplace, by where they went to school, then we want to consider only those West Indians who were born here, who went to school here, and who have either no accent or less of an accent than their parents. If in fact it has gotten more difficult with the second generation to tell the two groups apart, one should not find the second generation exhibiting the same kind of success that you find in the first. In reality, the second generation of West Indians have higher incomes than Anglo Saxons, and a higher percentage of people in the professions. If it is to be argued that a moral factor such as past slavery causes current black–white differentials in performance, then the differential should be even greater in the case of West Indians, whose experience under slavery was even worse than among blacks in the United States.

In the area of sex differences, there is also a whole moral vision with which most of you are probably already familiar. It holds that the male–female differences are the result of discrimination, that in recent times this has been fought and to some extent has been overcome. History is completely counter to that argument. The proportions of Ph.D.s, of M.D.s, of lawyers, of chemists, of economists who were female was much higher decades ago than it was in 1960. If you go back to 1905, the proportion of females in *Who's Who* was higher than it was in 1950. None of this fits the assumed pattern of discrimination. It is hard to believe that there was increasing discrimination over those decades, which led to the situation in 1960.

Demographic shifts are very highly correlated with the change. The age of marriage of college-educated women was constantly declining. The number of children born per white woman was increasing during that period. This decline in the representation of women in these various high-level occupations seems to have occurred across a broad front having nothing to do with male employers. It happened at women's colleges run by women deans, women department heads, and women presidents. There was, for example, an anguished letter in one of the Mount Holyoke alumnae magazines, written by a woman who came back for her twenty-fifth reunion. She recalled that when she was a student all the full professors and department heads were women. Now she finds that they are all men, even though the president of the college is still a woman. How can this be? It can be simply because the supply of women in those kinds of occupations declined relative to that of men, and that was true no matter whether the employer was male or female.

There are other and better indices. For example, in the case of women, the really crucial variable is whether they were ever married or not. If you look at female Ph.D.s who received their degrees in the 1930s and 1940s and calculate the percentage of them who became full professors by the 1950s, you find that women who never married became full professors to a greater extent than men over the same span of time. It is the women who married who met disaster. In most of the data, the real difference is not between men and women; it is between married women and all other persons. The married women tend to perform much worse than single women, particularly in high-level occupations that require continuous work and a great number of hours, occupations where you cannot go home and take care of your family very readily.

With men, it is just the opposite. It is the married man who outperforms the single man. There is nothing terribly mysterious or sinister about it, particularly for anyone who has ever been married and particularly for someone like myself who has been both married and divorced. I remember reading an article about divorced men that said, "You may notice that the house no longer magically cleans itself as it once used to do." You discover that you take your own laundry to the laundry and dry cleaning to the cleaners, and you do your own shopping in the market. When the kids have trouble with school you take off from work and you go to school and see about it, because your wife does not go to school to see about it anymore.

The issue of male–female employment patterns is a classic case of a problem that exists in the mind of intellectuals more so than in the reality of the world. The problem is that what is ascribed as the married man's income is in fact the income of two people, that is, the income is made possible by the joint activities of two people. The problem has been resolved in the real world. It is in the world of theory that it has not been resolved, because it is the man whose name appears on the check, and the statistics are collected that way. Those of us who are terribly worked up over these abstractions become terribly worked up over a problem that exists in those abstractions, but that does not necessarily reflect a problem in the real world. Some of the studies have tried to argue that it is not marriage that is so important, and they have various statistical breakdowns according to single women and single men to "prove" it. But "single" includes people who are widowed, divorced, and separated. Indeed, these constitute a substantial percentage of all single people. The crucial factor is people who were *never married.* When you look at academic women who were never married, they earn more than academic men who were never married.

USUAL SOLUTIONS TO THE PROBLEM OF POVERTY

Along with the "causes" of poverty you get many cures which, again, reflect the moral emphasis—and some self-interest as well. One finds education offered very often as a panacea by educators. When the Campbell Soup Company tells us how great it is to have soup for lunch, we tend to take that with a grain of salt. Yet when educators tell us the very same things about their products, we seem to think that they are public-spirited citizens trying nobly to solve our social problems.

There is a whole legend that has grown up around the history of the Jewish immigrants who came here poor and rose to affluence, supposedly through education. One of the problems is that high income groups do tend to have higher levels of education. They also tend to engage in high levels of travel and entertainment and own large homes. Yet no one would argue that travel, entertainment, or housing are the reasons or the ways by which one rises from poverty to affluence. A detailed study of the occupations of Jewish immigrants showed that they rose to affluence *first,* and then were able to afford to send their children to college. This is even more clear in the case of the Japanese immigrants on the West coast. Most of the Japanese were farmers as late as 1940, and most of them spoke very little English. But they were prosperous nonetheless, owning many businesses in California and Washington state. Because of this prosperity, they were able to send their children on to college, and then their children became better educated. But the education was not the cause of the rise.

One of the other cures of poverty is political reform. If you read many histories and discussions of social issues, you get the idea that the reason people are not in rags or hungry today is because various noble reformers refused to accept such conditions and worked to alleviate them. Meanwhile, it was just coincidental that the gross national product rose five or six times over that same span. But if you really want to know why it is that the poor of the nineteenth century were in rags and those of the twentieth century typically are not, it is because a man named Singer perfected the sewing machine, putting factory-made clothing within the reach of great masses of people for the first time in history. Prior to that time, either homemade or secondhand clothing was the standard dress for most working-class people. In addition to clothing the working class, secondhand garments also spread diseases throughout the whole society as they were passed around. Most working-class people in the nineteenth century could not afford the luxury of having shoes that were made differently for the right foot than for the left foot, until Singer made that economically feasible. In most parts of the world outside of the United States, working people could not afford shoes at all. In addition to Singer, there was something called the sweat shop on the lower East Side of New York that made that possible. It was not that we became too noble to allow it.

The fallacy of political reform as a solution to perceived social ills is that it ignores process and focuses only on results. The most fundamental problem in political decision making is that we cannot vote for a result; we can only vote for a process. We can *hope* for the result from that process. Some 50 to 60 years ago, prohibitionists felt that they were voting for a process that they hoped would end up eliminating the drinking of alcoholic beverages. They discovered the hard way, of course, that no such thing was possible. All sorts of other consequences resulted, including a tremendous increase in organized crime, under the influence of which we are still suffering. You cannot make political processes and market processes parallel by saying, "We vote with our dollars for this; why can't we vote with our ballots for that?" When we vote with our dollars, we vote for already produced results. We go into a showroom, and we look at the Chevy or Plymouth and decide whether we want to have it. We do not vote for the process by which it was produced because we do not know, and we are not required to know, what that process was. When we vote in politics we vote for a process, with *hope* that the end result of that process will be the things we want to have. Simply because the market mechanism has failed to produce the "optimal" result, it is by no means clear that political processes will then succeed. Unfortunately, it is usually a very short step from saying that the economic process will not decide this correctly to saying that the political process will. But, of course, the fact that you have proven that a fish cannot fly does not prove that a rhinoceros can.

WHAT CAN BE DONE

One tragic aspect of poverty policy is that the most productive thing the government could do to help is to stop making things worse. Unfortunately, such things as the dramatic increases in the minimum wage in the post World War II era are steps in the wrong direction. If you look at the black teenage unemployment rate in the 1970s, it is at least five times what it was as of around 1950. The argument is often made (again, the preference for the moralistic argument) that this increase is purely the result of racism. You cannot tell me that there was only one-fifth as much racism in 1950 as there was in 1970. If you look at the unemployment rate among blacks by age bracket, you find a very steep decline from the teenage years to about the mid to late twenties. These young people do not change color as they get older; they merely acquire more experience, and that brings down the unemployment rate. Blacks aged 25–45 have historically always had lower unemployment rates than whites under 25.

What has happened with the minimum wage is that since 1950 you have had an escalation in the amount of it and a spreading of the coverage. The minimum wage law was first passed in 1938, and immediately inflation was set off by World War II, so that the minimum level became absolutely irrelevant to the actual wage standard, which was way above that. It was the same as if there were no minimum wage law for most of the next decade and longer. By 1950, that began to change. Now, for the first time, there was an effective minimum wage and the coverage spread to new sectors. The initial coverage was about 43% of American workers, and for political reasons it was the better paid 43%. The political opposition was thus minimized by applying the minimum wage to people to whom it did not make any difference anyway. The employers would have less incentive to fight against it, because the employers in the affected industries were already paying more than the minimum. This is in keeping with the entering wedge theory of legislation. Once passed, the minimum wage law was then successively applied to more groups of employers. As a result, the *effective* coverage was really more than doubled in that period. Then the long-run consequence of that kind of law began to be felt. It is probably the most harmful single piece of social legislation on the books, as far as blacks are concerned—a tragic irony given that so much of the black leadership has fought for it and so much liberal political thought is in favor of it.

Improving the lot of the poor means enabling them to move up the ladder, but they have to get on the ladder before they can move up. The minimum wage law prevents that. It is playing double or nothing with someone else's life. The law says that if a person is valuable enough for the employer to pay $3.10 an hour, then he can be employed. If not, we deny him the right to work. We simply price him out of the market. There is a whole line of argument that says that people would only get "dead-end jobs" if there were no minimum wage legislation. But, of course, this is a misconception of the whole role of jobs and particularly of early jobs in one's career. What you learn on those jobs is how to get along on a job, with employers, with fellow workers. But you cannot learn these things if you are prevented from working at a wage commensurate with your limited productivity.

Sometimes the argument is made that government should be the employer of last resort. There is a great problem with that. If the government is going to impose the same kinds of standards that the private employer imposes, then the same people who are unemployed in the private market are going to be unemployable by the government. But government programs will "succeed," we may be sure of that. Therefore, there will be people employed in those programs, and if that requires the standards to change, so that people can be employed, then standards will be changed. Of course, what young workers are learning then is something completely counterproductive. They are learning that their behavior has much less effect upon their future than in fact it does, once they get out of a government job into the private market. This is extending into the job market the same kind of automatic promotion policies that exist in the school system. People are to be promoted not because of their performance, but because it is time to promote them. But this simply warps the novice worker's perception of the private labor market, and certainly does not aid in developing those attitudes necessary for success on the job.

JUSTICE AND FAIRNESS

In large part, our concern with moral factors and flirtation with status-based decisions enforced by government result from a deep-seated desire for a just society. Unfortunately, much of the discussion of justice proceeds as if we were God on Judgment Day. One of the small differences between intellectuals and God on Judgment Day is that God does not have to worry about what is going to happen the day *after* Judgment Day. We do. Our decisions have to be made in light of the fact that we must live with their consequences.

Let us imagine someone who has an ill-gotten fortune. We will assume he has acquired it by some method that was not illegal but that was clearly immoral. Some time in the past his ancestors landed on an island, murdered all the Indians, and took over. The island, which became a valuable property, has now come down through the family. In terms of current legality, it is legally his. We might talk about confiscating that fortune because of its immoral origin. But we have to think also what prospective results will come about from doing this. Clearly, if we are going to step in and confiscate property, not because of any illegality, but simply because of moral judgments on its history, then all property is subjected to great uncertainty, and declines in value immediately. It does not matter whether you ever planned, for example, to confiscate homes; all homes will fall under the onus of this increased risk. The present value of anything includes its future value, and that in turn is affected by the risk that it will be lost, partially or completely. Thus if you attempt the "just" solution, you will have confiscated part of the value of houses of people who have worked for decades to have homes for their families. More important than that, you will have created an incentive for people to keep their wealth in forms that the government will find hard to get hold of, to keep it in gold and silver and Swiss bank accounts instead of in factories and mines and other productive investments. The people who would end up most affected by this would be people who would be employed in the factories and the mines; people who do not own any fortunes may not own any homes, but nevertheless would be very adversely affected. The damage to them may have an economic value far exceeding that of the ill-gotten fortune.

Another example might be the existence of monarchy. You could, for example, ask what has someone done to be king, to have that kind of wealth and power. He may have done nothing. He *probably* has done nothing. But the more fundamental issue is, What are the costs and benefits of monarchy for the society at large, as compared to alternatives that are realistic for that society at the time and place where the decision is being made? That may be infinitely more important than whether this person who happens by accident of birth to be king gets a huge windfall gain or not. There are high social costs of trying to eliminate windfall gains.

Preoccupation with absolute justice often involves ignoring the future consequences of your action on people not defined in your original concern over justice. Adam Smith and John Rawls both said that justice is the paramount virtue of society, but they meant very different things. Smith's argument was that without *some* justice in the society, the society cannot survive. There cannot be a society without some predictability, and that predictability must be based on some principle and have some kind of consensus behind it. Rawls made the very different argument that every increment of justice was categorically more important than any increment of any other benefit.

It is very hard to see why you would be concerned about justice unless there were some value to the things that you were being just about. We are not going to get worked up over the fact that, when we leave the beach, we each go with different numbers of grains of sand in our hair, because we do not put any value on those grains of sand. For us even to be concerned about justice, there has to be some *prior* concern about the things that we are justly distributing or unjustly distributing. Once you say that A and B both have value, then it is hard to see how one can justify the statement that every increment of B must be more valuable than every increment of A, without regard to how large one is or how small the other might be. Yet, time after time, we take actions aimed at securing a bit more justice, with virtually no thought given to the costs of doing so. Once we admit that there are costs to justice, it is by no means clear that every increment of justice is desirable. Someone must pay those costs, and that undefined someone is no less important than those we have explicitly categorized and set in the center of our discussion.

An example of that sort of situation can be found in our experiences with "affirmative action." One of the tragedies about affirmative action is that there is very little empirical evidence that it has benefited blacks or women. Further there is reason to believe that it may be counterproductive. The equal opportunity laws (which were superseded by affirmative action) simply provided penalties for discrimination. The employer could avoid all penalties by not discriminating and incur penalties by doing so. It was a very straightforward incentive system. Affirmative action says something very different. Under affirmative action there are two sets of incentives created with respect to hiring and firing minorities.[1] The first incentive encourages employers to hire from

[1] Incidentally, the word "minorities" is to be taken with a considerable grain of salt. All the groups that are included for preferential treatment under affirmative action add up to two-thirds of the American population. So what affirmative action means in this context is that the government authorizes discrimination against one-third of the population—and, if you are a government contractor, it requires it.

these groups, because by doing so they will immediately get the government off their back. But down the road, employers are buying more trouble, because if the subsequent pay and promotion pattern of people hired from those groups does not meet the expectations of the government, then employers are incurring a very large legal process cost—regardless of whether they discriminated or not. There is no a priori reason to know which of these two incentives will be strongest. In some circumstances one might be stronger, in other circumstances the other might be stronger.

As a case in point, consider the academic world. Here you have an up-or-out system of promotion. A junior faculty member has to be either promoted or fired after a certain period of time. He cannot just be continued in that same rank. Under these circumstances, affirmative action increases the demand for those members of minority groups who have a proven track record, such that they will not have to be let go at the end of 3 or 4 years. This is particularly true of the large research universities, where it is common for a very large majority of all assistant professors to be let go at the end of their contract, and certainly not to be kept on for tenure positions. Universities are looking for qualities that no one knows how to determine in advance. What they do is get people out of the graduate schools who are regarded as being highly promising in a research sense, then they let them try out for 3 or 4 years. At the end of the trial period, the universities simply discard the losing bets and keep the winning bets. Given the nature of what they are looking for, it is fairly clear that perhaps only 10% of the people they hire are ever going to be retained. That is a system that was in existence long before people were concerned about discrimination problems. The people who were let go were let go, not for any fault of their own, not for any misdeeds, incompetence, or anything of that sort. It is just that what the university was looking for was something you cannot determine in advance.

Enter affirmative action. Are you now going to hire a woman who is fresh out of graduate school with a 9 out of 10 chance that you are going to fire her in 3 years, opening yourself for legal liability which can cost hundreds of thousands of dollars if she chooses to make a lawsuit out of it, whether or not you are found guilty? Affirmative action has created an incentive *not* to hire from these various groups, or to hire for administrative or similar positions which do not have the up-or-out dilemma. In the process, you have made those minority individuals who have top degrees and a lot of publications better off than they would have been otherwise, but they would have been doing all right anyway. Those who are coming out of the graduate school and are untested (and given the history of minorities, these will be the great majority of the people in the group) have been made more risky to hire than they were before. "Justice" has had a high cost to the intended beneficiaries, as well as to the larger society. Perhaps observers will be psychically benefited by feeling that they are promoting a more just world. But is increasing the psychic income of third parties the real purpose of income redistribution?

PART II

THE UNFORESEEN CONSEQUENCES OF REGULATION

CHAPTER 5

Is Mrs. Thatcher Curing the British Disease?

JOHN O'SULLIVAN

On my last visit to Britain, a newspaper headline caught my eye. It ran as follows: "Bolton Council last week closed down its nuclear bomb-proof shelter after it had been destroyed by vandals." That would make a marvellous introduction to a discussion of, say, British defense policy between the wars. Alas, there is no such neat joke summarizing the British disease, perhaps because that disease defies easy diagnosis.

On the surface, admittedly, the symptoms are clear enough. In 1945 the standard of living of the British people was matched in Europe only by Sweden and by Switzerland. Today, 11 other European nations are wealthier than the United Kingdom; the French and the West Germans are at least 40% better off. And in the near future, if current trends continue, Spain (a nation despised by the British a generation ago as backward and poverty-stricken) will surpass the United Kingdom in living standards. Until quite recently, moreover, British economic decline was only relative: We were getting richer; but we were not enriching ourselves as quickly as other people. But in the last decade,

The Limits of Government Regulation

ISBN 0-12-277620-8 0-12-277622-4(p)

Britain's economic performance, considered on its own, has begun to decline even in absolute terms. Between 1974 and 1979, our productivity growth was only .6% a year—the lowest since Britain pioneered the Industrial Revolution.

But, as Samuel Brittan—the doyen of British economic commentators—pointed out in his 1978 Henry Simon lecture at The University of Chicago,[1] this simplicity is something of an illusion. There are in fact *two* British diseases. The first is that, for over 100 years, Britain has had a lower rate of economic growth than other industrial economies. From 1879 to 1967 it had a growth rate of 1.3%; the average growth rate of 16 other industrial countries was 1.8%. Thus Britain's standard of living fell from second highest (Australia was the highest) 100 years ago, to its position today below most European countries.

But the second malaise is much more recent. Until about 15 years ago, Britain enjoyed very low rates of both inflation and unemployment. Since 1967, however, both have greatly increased. According to OECD figures, the average rise in the price level of industrialized countries between 1972 and 1977 was 60%; in Britain it was 120%. Unemployment, almost never above 2.5% until 1967, rose to 7% 10 years later, and is 10% of the labor force today.

Some observers such as Bernard Nossiter, author of *Britain: A Future That Works,*[2] argue that this is more than compensated for by the civilized and agreeable atmosphere of life in Britain. He believes that the British have sensibly chosen a civilized mixture of modest affluence and greater leisure in contrast to the mad strivings for more of lesser breeds without the law of diminishing returns. His argument reminds me of a line from Chesterton: "He has eyes that see things that other men cannot see—the eyes of a mystic or of a house agent." For that "civilized and agreeable atmosphere" is less and less in evidence as the disease becomes more

[1] Reprinted in *The Journal of Law and Economics,* University of Chicago Law School, October 1978.

[2] B. Nossiter, *Britain: A Future That Works* (Boston: Houghton Mifflin Co., 1978).

acute. Economic decline in Britain has in turn produced social discontent and increasing social conflict. There is a simple reason for this. When an economy produces more wealth every year, all of the social groups can obtain more without necessarily raiding one another's kitty. But when the economic pie is shrinking in size, social groups can only get more by attempting to take something from others.

My evidence for this is the character of the trade union disturbances during the winter of 1979, which must have achieved some sort of a record in unpleasantness. Strikes were widespread throughout the country, and produced such celebrated tourist attractions as rubbish piling up in Leicester Square. In Liverpool, even the gravediggers went on strike! But far worse were the frequent instances of extraordinary callousness. In one case, two ambulance men were picking up a crippled man to take to the hospital. As they were bringing him from the house to the ambulance, over the radio came the news that an ambulance drivers' strike had been declared, whereupon they left the crippled man *helpless in the snow*—a scene that a writer of Victorian melodrama would scarcely have dared to invent.

What are the causes of this variegated British disease? Let me first get some false explanations out of the way. It is not caused by either Britain's rigid class system or by the loss of the British Empire. With respect to the first, Americans have got hold of a very misguided notion in this vision of a rigid British class structure. They seem to take quite literally the story of the upper-class army officer who returned from the battle of Dunkirk and, when asked what it was like, replied: "My dear, the noise, *the people*." In fact, Britain has always been socially a very mobile society. About two-fifths of people end up in a social class different from that occupied by their parents—a figure very similar to that in the United States and in Australia, and much higher than in continental European countries. Only a quarter of managers and professionals have fathers from the same background. A greater proportion come from the families of manual laborers. In addition, more working-class children attend university in Britain than in almost all other continental European countries. Nor is this just a recent trend. As Peter Bauer has reminded us, a study of a cotton industry before 1914 (carried out ironically by Sidney Webb, the Fabian socialist) showed that two-thirds of senior managers had started out either as shop floor workers or as lowly clerks.[3] Then again, if we look at British politics, we see that people from humble origins have succeeded remarkably down the years. Lloyd George, an orphan brought up by his shoemaker uncle, became prime minister in 1916. Ramsey McDonald, the first Labour prime minister, was the illegitimate son of a poor Scottish girl. Tories too have risen from the ranks. Edward Heath was the son of a housemaid and a jobbing carpenter. Mrs. Thatcher herself, the daughter of a lower-middle-class shopkeeper, made her way in the world by scholarships and hard work. Even the British Army prior to World War I, which you might suppose would be a socially frozen zone, demonstrates that merit enabled people to rise. Field Marshall Sir William Robertson, Chief of the Imperial General Staff, joined the army as a private and worked his way up from the ranks, becoming CIGS just before World War I. He always dropped his "aitches." So British society is less a case of "Upstairs Downstairs" and more a case of what Bernard Shaw called upstarts and downstarts.

Why, then, is there the widespread belief in the opposite view? Perhaps the surface appearance of British society, with its titles and decorations, its upper-class festivities such as Ascot and Henley, gives this false impression. But remember that titles and decorations are often the reward of economic success. Ogden Nash, the American poet, put this point well when he said, "In America, a rich butter and egg man is simply a rich butter and egg man, but in England he is Sir Benjamin Buttery, Bart."

The second erroneous explanation is that the decline of Britain has been produced by the loss of empire. It is argued by many, following Lenin and the English economist Hobson, that the

[3] P. T. Bauer, "Class on the Brain," Centre for Policy Studies, London, 1978.

British benefited from exploiting colonies, from the super-profits of colonial investments, and from selling goods to colonial captive markets. Again, that is not supported by the evidence. In places like the Third World it is an attractive idea, because it provides an excuse for their present economic failure. But if we look at the facts, we find little support for that idea. To begin with, there were no captive markets as such during most of the heyday of the British Empire, which was run on the theory of free trade. Other countries could and did sell in colonial markets. Nor was British trade dependent solely on colonial markets. In 1914, for instance, India was the single largest market for British goods, but Imperial Germany was the *second* largest market.

Finally, there were no "super-profits" to be had from colonial investments. An investor could get a much better return on his money by investing in either North or Latin America, which Britain did not control politically. Peter Duignan of the Hoover Institute points out that, by contrast, the profits on British investments in Africa were usually very low. One of the biggest overseas companies, The British South Africa Company, which virtually ran Rhodesia, *took 26 years before declaring a single dividend.*

On the other side of the ledger, there was a distinct economic cost to Britain in running the Empire. People with good degrees from Oxbridge, whom we would nowadays call "the best and the brightest," did not go into industry. They went into the Indian Civil Service or the Colonial Office. This represented a considerable diversion of talent away from Britain and the United Kingdom economy toward other societies. In short, it is highly questionable whether imperialism is a good way of making money. Look, for example, at Europe. Its two most prosperous countries, Sweden and Switzerland, had no significant colonies; whereas Portugal, with a large and extensive colonial empire until the day before yesterday, is one of the poorest nations in Western Europe. It is possible that, far from explaining Britain's economic success in the past and its failure now, the British Empire makes that early success all the more surprising. British colonialism might be better described as a gigantic exercise in philanthropy that was supported by previous economic success.

What, then, are the real causes of the British disease? We should look first at the question of investment. Critics sometimes argue that U.K. investment has been too low in the post-war world. In fact, it has been average: the same as West Germany's, higher than U.S. investment, but lower than Japan's. What has been low is the *quality* of investment. A Confederation of British Industry study of manufacturing investment from 1958 to 1972 concluded that, for every unit of investment, the West Germans achieved twice the increase of output in Britain, the United States 50% more, the Japanese 70% more, etc. Rates of return on capital investment show a similar pattern. Only Italy has a record as bad as Britain's, though Sweden is catching up (or, more accurately, down).

One reason is that, in the United Kingdom, investment is strongly influenced by the government. To begin with, a great deal of investment is direct state investment. David Ramsey Steele, a young U.K. economist, recently examined the percentage of total investment accounted for by the central government, local authorities, and nationalized industries. Between 1969 and 1979, it fluctuated between 32 and 44%. We might, therefore, conclude that, as a rule of thumb, state investment is equal to 38% of total investment in any one year.

Even in the prosperous 1950s, the evidence was clear that public sector investment was less productive than private. George and Priscilla Polanyi calculated that nationalized industry investment enjoyed a rate of return only half that of the private sector. In the harsher economic climate of 1979, a sum equal to the government revenue from North Sea oil was spent on subsidies to such loss-making ventures as British Steel, British Shipbuilders, and British Leyland.

Even ostensibly private investment, however, is subject to great government influence. Since the 1960s, the British government has erected a vast array of subsidies and controls to direct private investment from its most economically advantageous applications to disadvantaged regions in order to achieve wider social purposes such as the equalization of income levels in different regions. Thus, for example, Rootes Motors was directed to Scotland and to bankruptcy. But the wider social purposes must have been generally elusive because, by the last election, the regions judged to be disadvantaged had grown to 66% of Britain's geographical area and to 40% of the British labor force.

One need not be a cynic to realize why investment is directed by the government to applications which are unprofitable and perhaps permanently loss-making. Under conditions of democracy, politicians have an interest in preserving declining industries because they are full of constituents with votes. By definition no one works in plants in industries which cannot be built because of this diversion of capital.

The second major cause of the British disease is the power of labor unions. For even when investment is sensibly directed, labor unions in Britain have the power—and use it—to ensure that the investment will not result in more efficient working practices. Their tactics include make-work restrictions, barriers to movement between related trades, working rules that increase costs, the prevention of cost-reducing innovations, etc. They are, in fact, more damaging than strikes and walk-outs to an industry's long-term prosperity. And they are long established in the United Kingdom. In the 1975 report, *The Future of the Car Industry*, the Central Policy Review Staff (which is the British government's own "think tank") concluded that even when assembling the same car, and working with identical capital equipment, nearly twice as many men were required in British plants as in Japanese or European ones. The work pace was slower due to slower production line speeds, late starts, frequent stoppages, and bad work practices. Maintenance was also poor. British plants employed 50 to 70% more maintenance men than continental European plants, yet lost twice as many production hours due to break-downs.

Three years after this pessimistic report came out, Stephen Fay of *The Sunday Times* inquired into labor relations in the continental and British plants of the Ford Motor Company. The company produced the same cars on the same machines in a number of countries. *The only major variable factor was labor,* yet in 1978 it took 9.5 Britons to build an Escort at Halewood and only 4.1 West Germans at the Saarlouis plant. One British worker at Dagenham produced 110 doors for Cortinas, while a Belgian worker at Genk produced 240. Bernard Passingham, the leading Transport and General Workers steward at Dagenham, talked of a press in the plant that had not been worked for 7 years because the workers considered the machine unsafe. Another machine, which cost $2.6 million, stood idle for 8 months while the stewards negotiated manning levels.

But why should the Ford Motor Company tolerate in Britain working practices that would horrify it elsewhere? The unique legal privileges of labor unions are what make Britain different and companies reluctant to attempt to install more efficient practices and labor-saving machinery. For practical purposes, a British labor union cannot be sued. Enjoying complete immunity for torts "alleged to have been committed by or on behalf of the trade union" (1906 Trades Disputes Act), they can break contracts, libel opponents, conduct boycotts, blockade third parties uninvolved in the original dispute, and inflict all kinds of economic damage on employers, their own members, and the general public with no fear of their victims seeking legal redress. These unique legal advantages mean that very heavy economic costs can be imposed by a union on any employer who risks industrial trouble in order to improve the firm's efficiency. The employer would in all probability lose more in the course of the dispute than he or she could hope to gain by its successful outcome. In such a legal environment, continued inefficiency and overmanning make good economic sense.

What, however, of the economic environment? In particular, what of taxation? It is a myth—though an understandable one—that Britain is very highly taxed in comparison with other industrial countries. The British are *among* the most highly taxed nations, fourth in a list of 17 industrial countries. But in 1975, they paid as much as the West Germans, less than the Swedes, more than the Americans. Where Britain is really exceptional is in its very high marginal rates of tax on higher incomes. Until the Budget of 1979, British taxpayers paid a 50% tax on incomes of about $22,000; and at incomes of just over $50,000, those who received salaries paid 83% and those whose incomes were derived from savings and investment paid the confiscatory rate of 98%!

Such unrealistically high rates were bound to produce perverse economic behavior. There was, most obviously, a marked incentive to leisure and a disincentive to work. Here, as Paul Craig Roberts has argued,[4] is the economic basis of the supposed "leisure preference" of the British worker as celebrated by Bernard Nossiter. Tax shelters, too, proliferated. Talented people were accordingly diverted into the essentially barren activity of investing schemes of tax avoidance. Emigration rates, moreover, were high and rising. And capital has been consumed rather than invested in the future. Why do the supposedly impoverished British have so many Rolls-Royce automobiles on the streets of London? Suppose a rich man, earning over $50,000 a year, had $60,000 to invest. Were he to obtain an annual rate of return of, say, 15%, this would give him $9,000 a year. But the tax rate of 98% prevailing until 1979 would have reduced this to a mere $180. On the other hand, an expenditure of $60,000 would have given him a magnificent Rolls-Royce to carry him around town and impress his fellows. And the real cost to him of this lordly pleasure would have been a mere $180, that is, the foregone earnings from investing his money.

A final contributory factor to the British disease is high public spending. Of the various methods of measuring public spending as

[4] "Decline and Restoration; Pointers from the British," *Washington Quarterly*, Autumn 1980, Georgetown Center for Strategic and International Studies.

a percentage of national income, all show a secular rise in the last 20 years. The measure most commonly used put public spending at 42% of the gross domestic product (gdp) in 1978. Other countries, of course, have high rates of public spending without suffering the specific economic difficulties of the United Kingdom. But there are two factors in the British case which help to account for its damaging effects.

The first is that a smaller percentage of public spending in Britain is accounted for by transfer payments than elsewhere. Publicly provided services and nationalized industries correspondingly take a larger share of the total. Thus, between 1960 and 1976, United Kingdom public sector employment rose very sharply by over 1.5 million workers when the total labor force rose by only 1 million. This is significant because, as many studies have shown, services provided by the public sector are relatively wasteful and inefficient compared to the private sector. The employment shift from the private to the public sector is thus in itself a sign of increasing inefficiency. Transfer payments, by contrast, have no such direct economic effect.

Second, the rise in public spending since the middle 1960s, though erratic, has been very substantial. Such spurts obviously create difficulties when the government attempts to finance them. Broadly speaking, there are three methods of financing government spending—taxation, with which we have already dealt, borrowing, and inflation. In recent years, the public sector borrowing requirement (PSBR), which is Mandarin English for the government deficit, has risen to very high levels. In 1975 it reached the figure of 12% of the gross national product. Extravagant borrowing of this order tends both to raise interest rates and to "crowd out" borrowing by private industry. There is thus a constant temptation for governments to avoid this problem (temporarily) by financing their program through the creation of money. This was essentially the method chosen by the Heath Government in 1972–1974 when the money supply was increased by figures approaching 20% per annum. Hardly surprisingly, this led to the great inflation of 1975 when inflation reached an annual rate of 25%.

These, then, are the causes of Britain's two related economic diseases. But an immediate objection arises: Are not many of these policies and institutions present in countries which have a far healthier economic record than Britain's? Nossiter, in his book, has some fun pointing out, rightly, that the Swedes pay higher taxes, the Germans have a larger public sector, the French have more industrial intervention, etc. But Britain is peculiar in exhibiting a high level of state intervention in almost every area. It is as if the Tory tradition of paternalistic authority had mated with Labour's ideology of Fabian bureaucracy to produce the typical British office-holder, permanently in power—the gentleman collectivist. As a result, the Swedes have less nationalization, the Germans less state direction of investment, the Americans lower taxes,. . . .

Mr. Brittan, in his Henry Simon lecture, puts the same point more precisely, if also cautiously: "A generalization worth considering is that you can have a great deal of state intervention, or a high level of egalitarian social policy, but not both."

The analysis of Britain's problems just presented differs only slightly and in detail from the argument presented in the 1979 election by Mrs. Thatcher and the Tory Party. But, after 2 years of Tory Government, the following question must be asked: Will Mrs. Thatcher attempt to carry out her announced policies of reducing public expenditure and the size of the state, cutting taxes, slimming down subsidies to both nationalized and private industry, and reforming the unique legal privileges of the trade unions? This question must come as something of a surprise to those who are under the innocent impression that Mrs. Thatcher, under the fearsome guise of "Attila the Hen," has been ruthlessly imposing these policies on a nervous country, a cowed Civil Service, and a queasy Cabinet. Indeed, they may even have the vague feeling that these policies have not only been tried but have in addition failed rather spectacularly, thus repudiating in their collapse the views of Professor Milton Friedman, the *Wall Street Journal* editorial page, President Reagan, and assorted opponents of collectivism around the globe.

The appropriate conclusion to draw from this is that most reports in the American press about the "Thatcher experiment" have been inaccurate to the point of fiction. A typical example: Anthony Holden in the *New Republic* (January 26, 1981), pronounced confidently: "Mrs. Thatcher's election promises in 1978–1980; reduce government spending, eliminate waste, cut back the bureaucracy, tighten control of the money supply. For all of Thatcher's patent sincerity in applying what she thought appropriate, if painful, remedies, none of them has worked." If this passage means that Mrs. Thatcher actually did reduce state spending, tighten control of the money supply, etc., then it is simply false. As we shall see later in greater detail, public spending has increased and control of the money supply has been loosened since May 1979. This makes nonsense of Holden's claim that "none of them has worked." None of what? The rhetorical pledge or the actual policies? The great flaw of American reporting has been to concentrate on the speeches of Tory Ministers in praise of free enterprise and "monetarism" without examining if their words were reflected in statistics of public expenditure, taxation, and monetary growth. As Friedman has cautioned many times, one must watch what is *done* not what is *said*.

When once those grim records are inspected, a very different picture emerges. Let us first examine the Government's monetary policy or what critics are pleased to call "Mrs. Thatcher's dogmatic adherence to monetarism." It is certainly true that both Mrs. Thatcher and the Chancellor of the Exchequer, Sir Geoffrey Howe, came into office convinced that inflation was a monetary phenomenon and determined to reduce it by a gradual winding down of the rate of increase of the money supply. It is equally true that, in March 1980, the Chancellor set target growth rates for the money supply for the following 4 years. But there the dogmatic adherence ends.

Target rates and good intentions notwithstanding, the money supply has lunged out of control. Last year, for instance, the target for M3 (which is its total of notes and coins in circulation plus sterling bank deposits) was for an increase within the range 7–11%. The actual growth rate was 20%, which, even after allowance had been made for special factors, remained high at 17.5%.

Admittedly, other monetary indicators suggested that the money supply had in fact been restrained. On this explanation, the weather had improved in line with meteorological forecasts, but the barometer in question was inaccurate. Some support for this view can be seen in the depressed state of the British economy which has all the marks of a monetary squeeze (although, as we shall see, there are other explanations of this). We should properly be cautious about such arguments, however, since they were precisely the excuses offered by defenders of Heath's monetary expansion in 1973. Moreover, M3 is the Government's own chosen target figure. It has reiterated this standard in the latest Budget of March 1981, and set new targets for M3. So, until M3 begins to show an improvement in line with their forecasts, we cannot say that the money supply is under control, let alone being steadily reduced.

The reasons for this failure are interesting and undermine, among other criticisms, Galbraith's contention that Friedmanite monetarism is at the bottom of Britain's economic troubles. Of the various techniques of monetary control, the one most favored by orthodox monetarists is control of the monetary base. But this method was firmly opposed by Treasury civil servants, who have always been skeptics about monetarism of any kind and regard monetary base control as the extreme form of the heresay. Opposition also came from the Governor of the Bank of England, who is a sort of closet Keynesian. Under this pressure the Government selected instead the much more complex technique of controlling five different determinants of credit, notably interest rates and the public sector borrowing requirement (PSBR). Of this method Friedman said in a written submission in June 1980 to a committee of MP's:

> I could hardly believe my eyes when I read the first paragraph of the summary chapter (of *Monetary Control,* the Government's Green Paper on monetary policy, published in March 1980): "The principal means of controlling the growth of the money supply must be fiscal policy—both public expenditure and tax policy—and interest rates." Interpreted literally, this sentence is simply wrong. Only a Rip Van Winkle, who has not read any of the flood of literature during the past decade and more on the money supply process, could possibly have written that sentence.

Another orthodox monetarist, Michael Parkin, in a Mont Pelerin paper delivered in September 1980 (to which I am much indebted), went even further and described the Government's chosen method as "a technique which is almost guaranteed to fail." Of the many difficulties with this form of monetary control, perhaps the most important is that, as the Green Paper itself admitted, "It is impossible to forecast the PSBR . . . and very difficult to control it closely."

That has turned out to be a vast understatement. The original March 1980 forecast of the PSBR, on which the monetary target was in part based, was for a deficit of $20.4 billion. By November 1980, it had been revised to $27.6 billon or about 5% of Britain's gross domestic product (GDP). And by the time of the March Budget, it had risen to $30 billion. In short, the government deficit, which is the centerpiece of the policy for controlling the money and thereby gradually bringing down inflation, has itself proved unamenable to control—throwing the entire monetary strategy out of kilter, as orthodox monetarists warned from the first.

Why, however, has the government deficit bolted out of control? This can be traced directly to what most commentators (and even some Ministers) now agree is the Government's most serious economic error—its failure, despite four bites at the cherry since May 1979, to cut state spending. Does this again surprise those who may have read about "savage cuts" in public spending with heart-rending stories of nursery schools being shut down for lack of staff? The first point to grasp is that, under the regime of long-term planning of public expenditure, something counts as a "cut" if it is a reduction in the amount allocated to be spent in some future spending program. Essentially, such "cuts" are merely disappointed aspirations. And since Labour left behind inordinately optimistic spending plans, conceived with the 1979 election in mind, it was possible to "cut" savagely without touching any existing programs whatsoever.

That is not, however, a firm guarantee against nursery school closures or the abandonment of half-built municipal swimming pools. Bureaucrats in both town halls and Whitehall are quick to ensure that, whatever else is sacrificed to economy, it will not be their jobs or the size of their bureaus. Hence, in the series of public spending cuts since 1975, overall government expenditure remained static while capital spending was cut by 50%. The ironic result has been that the jobs axed by "cuts" have been largely in the private sector, among construction and manufacturing companies supplying the government. Otherwise, more and more public sector workers have administered worse and worse services.

Even so, the Government's savagery was very modest. It proposed merely to "stabilize" public spending for the years 1979–1981, and then to reduce it year-by-year to achieve a 4% real reduction in public spending by 1984. What made this grand project dubious was the convenient arrangement of the cuts: minor piffling cuts proposed in the here-and-now; large reductions confidently forecast for the never-never land of 1983–1984. And this skepticism was reinforced by the political fate of the immediate spending reductions sought by Mrs. Thatcher and her political allies among cabinet Ministers. In the July 1979 discussions, Mrs. Thatcher and Sir Geoffrey originally asked for spending reductions amounting to $19.2 billion; the compromise that emerged from the Cabinet was a mere $8.4 billion. Still more significant was the Cabinet discussion of expenditure reductions in November 1980. Here the Treasury, with the full backing of the prime minister, demanded $4.8 billion worth of cuts. It was sent away with a flea in its ear and agreed cuts of only half that figure—namely $2.4 billion. This represented a real check both to prime ministerial power in general and to Mrs. Thatcher's direction of economic policy in particular.

If cuts were small, however, unanticipated rises in current government costs were large. The most striking example in 1979–1980 was the sharp increase in the public sector wage bill. This was the result of lavish pay awards determined by a special commission, set up by the Labour Government on its deathbed and chaired by the leftish Hugh Clegg, which operated on the assumption that public sector workers should be paid on the basis of "comparability" with the private sector but without adjusting for the absence of risk, indexed pensions, and similar nonwage benefits enjoyed by the public sector employee. According to official estimates, these pay rises added $4.8 billion to public spending in a full year. But dry the starting tear! This was a case of a very large chicken flapping home to roost. Mrs. Thatcher herself had promised to honor the Clegg awards on the straightforward political calculation that to do otherwise might lose the votes of public sector workers.

In the financial year, 1980–1981, public spending was sharply increased by the higher-than-expected rise in unemployment. Every 100,000 people who lost their jobs in the private sector added approximately $1.2 billion to the PSBR, as income receipts fell and social benefits were paid out. (Public sector unemployment creates a slight surplus to the exchequer—but there has not been much of that.) Again, Sir Geoffrey Howe estimated that the recession had caused in this way about half of the unexpected increase in the government deficit—which means, of course, that half the deficit is due to "other factors." These boil down to the failure, described above, to compel the spending ministries to control their budgets.

The net result of all this is that, by every possible test—in constant prices, in money terms, in volume, as a percentage of national income—*public spending has increased under the Tories.* The increase in real terms is admittedly modest, between 1 and 2%. But, since throughout this period national income has been falling, public spending has been taking a significantly larger share of it. According to Budget figures, public spending as a percentage of GDP rose from 41.5% under Labour to 44.5% in mid 1981.

Since Mrs. Thatcher is not a supply-sider, this failure to control public spending dictated a cautious policy of overall tax increases. It is true that, in line with election pledges, the 1979 budget cut the standard rate of income tax by 3% and the highest rate from 83% on earned income, and 98% on investment income, to 60% and 75% respectively. But this *largesse* had to be financed by sharp increases in consumption taxes in the 1979 budget. Since then, tax rates have risen and continue to rise. Sir Geoffrey's latest budget (March 1981) represents a strategic decision to finance the swollen public spending by taxation rather than by borrowing. Thus, the PSBR, which was forecast to rise in 1981–1982 to $37 billion if policies had been unchanged, is cut by $10 billion to $24 billion (as to 4.3% of GDP). At the same time, taxation was increased by $11 billion—almost the same amount. Some indication of the trend can be gathered from the statistics of total state revenue (i.e., tax revenue plus charges for state services, etc.). As a percentage of national income, state revenue rose from 41.3% under Labour to 43.3% in the first 6 months of 1980. Since then it has risen still further.

So much for the macro-economic legends! But what of other aspects of economic and industrial policy? Here at least the Thatcher Government can boast some modest achievements. It has abolished the Price Commission, which had administered price control since 1972 through the period of the largest rise in prices in British history. It has taken a few tentative and nervous steps in the direction of "privatizing" some of the nationalized industries—selling the hotel subsidaries of British Rail and making provision for the sale of shares in British Airways (though not as yet putting the shares on the market). Should this policy ever extend beyond trivial gestures, it would subject the nationalized industries to the disciplines of the capital market (but, as we shall see, that is light years away). There has been "Lakerization" of the long-haul bus routes, which has brought fares tumbling down as mini-bus owners rushed to compete with established operators. And one economic reform should especially appeal to people of a libertarian outlook: Sir Geoffrey Howe abolished at a stroke the system of exchange control that since 1939 had placed severe restrictions on the right of British citizens to invest abroad or even to take out money when emigrating.

Against these modest successes, however, must be set two major failures of nerve. These are associated, oddly enough, with the Government's two most controversial Ministers—Sir Keith Joseph in the Industry Department and James Prior at Employment.

Sir Keith entered office with the reputation of a born-again monetarist who had publicly repented his statist and Keynesian sins in past public office and announced that, although a Tory politician for over 20 years, he had "only recently become a Conservative." In Opposition, he ranged up and down the country preaching the gospel of sound money, private enterprise, the signaling function of prices, the folly of state control of investment, the futility of job subsidies and aid to "lame duck" companies, and more in like vein. For every unprofitable job temporarily shored up by subsidies, he argued, another worthwhile job is destroyed through the burden of the extra taxation or borrowing needed to finance the subsidy. He called this process "Dracula economics."

But in office, Sir Keith has been born yet again, this time as a statist tycoon. In the disillusioned words of one Tory MP, "He wrings his hands and pays out." There was some early talk, for instance, of gradually withdrawing subsidies to nationalized industries to force them to compete. But the figures (in constant prices) for nationalized industry external financing show a spectacular increase. Labour's last full year, 1978–1979, had expenditures under this heading of $5.7 billion. In the first year of Sir Keith's tutelage, the sum rose to $6.3 billion. At the time of the March budget it was planned that the figures for 1980–1981 would be almost stabilized at just over $6.3 billion. But, during the year, various nationalized industries got into such dire financial straits that the "cash limits" on their borrowing had to be raised by $1.4 billion to $7.7 billion—an increase of almost a third on Labour's total.

British Steel is a dramatic illustration of how the problem of nationalized industries gradually draws Ministers from the path of financial virtue. In 1979–1980, subsidies to the British Steel Corporation amounted to $1.7 billion. The target figure of $1.08 billion was laid down for 1980–1981. Indeed the government fought the steel strike to resist union demands for relaxation of these financial constraints. But faced by the prospect of the BSC simply unable to pay its bills, Sir Keith has since added another $1 billion in subsidies—to make a grand total of $2.3 billion for 1980–1981. Here is more evidence for Mrs. Thatcher's clear-sighted analysis in the halcyon days of Opposition: "We don't own the nationalized industries; the nationalized industries own us."

Scarcely less dramatic is the history of British Leyland, which, from its nationalization in 1975 up to 1979, had received $2.9 billion from the taxpayer. Another $720 million was added in 1980 with the usual threats that this represented One Last Chance. On the 27th of January 1981, however, Sir Keith announced a further infusion of $2.4 billion over the next 2 years. To get some idea of the magnitude of this industrial support, consider that the sums spent on British Leyland and British Steel are together roughly equal to the forecast government revenue from North Sea oil in the next financial year. This *largesse* also makes nonsense of, for instance, Leonard Downie's claim in the *Washington Post* (February 1, 1981) that Mrs. Thatcher's policies represent "the survival of the fittest."

We must seek the explanation in politics rather than economics. It is politically very difficult to resist the clamor for subsidies in time of recession. Commentators argue that the alternative to a subsidy is the bankruptcy of the company which they interpret not as the reallocation of resources, but as their vanishing into thin air, leaving all its employees (and *every* employee of *any* firm that *ever* provided it with goods and services, albeit only a spanner) permanently unemployed. If the government initially contests this logic, marches are held, Sir Keith hanged in effigy or personally splattered with tomatoes, parliamentary debates suspended following disorders (Labour cries of "Shame," "Resign," "Butcher," "Suez," etc.) and Tory "Wets" (an old Tory term, originally meaning weak or appeasing, now signifying moderate opposition to Mrs. Thatcher's supposed "hard-line") worry publicly about the dangers of social unrest. Eventually the money is paid out.

The second failure of nerve was the Government's decision, after much internal wrangling, to implement only very modest changes in labor union legislation. It was not, however, Mr. Prior's nerve that failed. As the leading Tory Wet, he had consistently fought for only minor and cosmetic reforms acceptable to the leadership of the Trades Union Congress (TUC). It was the Prime Minister and the Chancellor of the Exchequer who favored more stringent legislation.

There were three principal bones of contention—the closed shop, secondary picketing (i.e., picketing outside a factory by people who worked elsewhere), and the secondary boycott in general. The legislative hawks objected to these practices on two grounds. It was held to be offensive to civil liberty that a man might lose his job, and in unionized professions, his very prospect of employment, simply for refusing to join a labor union. Likewise, why should a union be allowed by law to inflict economic penalties on a company in pursuit of its dispute with another company? The second ground was economic efficiency. It was indeed linked to the argument from civil liberty since practices like secondary picketing and closed shop were believed to greatly strengthen labor unions against employers. And what had they done with this augmented strength? The hawks argued, as I did above, that they had enforced over-manning and restrictive practices on British industries leading to the waste of investment (that was often mistaken in the first place).

Prior's opposition to these arguments was generally interpreted by an indulgent press as large-hearted liberalism. A more accurate characterization would be that he was kowtowing to the big battalions. Thus, he would sometimes defend the closed shop on the grounds that both unions and management saw it as a way of ensuring that bargains would be kept. Less delicately, the unions would have the power to sack offenders against collective agreements. But this seemingly hard-headed argument failed to take into account the tradition of respect for militancy within which union leaders act. How often do unions expel wild-cat strikers who refuse to follow instructions from headquarters? Almost never. Yet they invariably punish blacklegs, usually by expulsion. There are even cases on record of unions allowing local branches to fine or expel members who, in deference to official union instructions, had remained at work during a local unofficial strike!

Battle was joined on these points in a discreet and even secretive fashion. Prior outlined his exceedingly modest proposals in Cabinet and Cabinet committees and, with the support of other such "Wets" as Lord Hailsham and the Deputy Prime Minister, Mr. Whitelaw, won the day in those councils. Defeated here, Mrs. Thatcher sought to subvert her colleague's plans in more indirect ways. With her encouragement and assistance, Sir Geoffrey Howe delivered a major speech declaring that it would be "fatal to Britain's chances if this government lost its nerve and neglected its clear duty to take in hand the necessary reform of the law." Ministerial emissaries began to arrive at the office of newspaper editors, hinting that they spoke for the Prime Minister and urging strong editorial criticism of the Prior legislation. Likely critics of the legislation were approached by junior Ministers, personally loyal to the Prime Minister, and asked to denounce it in heavyweight letters to the press. All to no avail. Mr. Prior kept his nerve and his critics abandoned theirs.

The Act that eventually reached the Statute Book was accordingly so mild that it deserved the name of opinion rather than law. It subjected future closed shops to the test of 80% support in a ballot of employees; but it left all existing closed shops intact. It allowed employers to bring injunctions against named pickets in certain cases of unlawful secondary picketing, but it did not oblige pickets to give their names. Mr. Prior's recent guidelines on possible future legislation, moreover, argue against giving police the power to require names from pickets in case it casts doubt on police neutrality in industrial disputes. And, finally, in a hitherto murky area of law the Act created an actual *right* of secondary boycott in drawing a distinction between legitimate secondary action against immediate suppliers and customers and unlawful action against remote suppliers and customers. In all other respects, trade unions retain their rights to break contracts, libel opponents, conduct secondary boycotts, and inflict all kinds of economic damage on employers and the general public, still with no fear of their victims seeking legal redress or of union funds being at risk.

It is peculiarly accurate to describe this as the result of a failure of nerve. For the argument that swayed Cabinet and backbench doubters alike was that, however justified more stringent legislation might be, such laws would simply not be accepted by large numbers of unionists and, consequently, could not be enforced. The argument cannot be dismissed out of hand. Labor unions have successfully defined unwelcome laws in the past. On the other hand, the vast majority of unionists are law-abiding people. And opinion polls have shown for some years that union members support much more severe restraints on unions than are contained in the Prior Act. It must, therefore, be a matter of judgment as to whether there would have been enthusiastic support among union members for a campaign of resistance to new laws in the particular circumstances of 1980. In retrospect a great opportunity for reform seems to have been thrown away. At the best of times labor unionists are reluctant to strike for political objectives, or indeed for any objectives apart from higher wages. However, 1980 has not been the best of times. Factories have been closing down and men have been laid off. Anxiety about the economic future is pervasive. Union militancy has shrivelled in this cold climate, and the number of strikes has fallen considerably from earlier years. Would union members have put their jobs at risk in order to fend off laws that a majority of them favored in the first place? Surely not. In which case it is a mark of the Tory Cabinet's timidity that it was unprepared to take even so modest a gamble on the side of its own convictions.

In general and in detail, therefore, Mrs. Thatcher's policies are quite different from the mythical Thatcherism denounced by Galbraithian and journalistic critics. But what of the actual economic consequences of Mrs. Thatcher? Is there a similar chasm between report and reality? Here the answer must be that, while Britain's economy is in serious recession, there is not the unrelieved economic disaster that some critics detect. What is wrong can be easily stated. Production is down and falling; bankruptcies are at record levels; unemployment has reached a post-war high of 10% of the employed population; and most forecasts predict that these conditions will worsen in 1981.

But there are also unmistakable shoots of economic improvement thrusting up through the gloom. The most heartening is the rate of inflation. After reaching a peak of almost 22% in May 1980, it has come down to a year-on-year rate of 13 in February 1981. Caroline Atkinson of the *Washington Post* (February 1, 1981) sniffed skeptically at this: ". . . the British inflation rate is slowing (although it is still higher than when Thatcher took office)." Atkinson is determined not to be comforted. For the inflation rate when Labour lost power was rising rapidly, whereas today it is falling fast. In the 6 months up to February, for instance, it had risen at an annualized rate of only 7%.

Almost as interesting as the bare figure is the composition of inflation. The reduction has been achieved almost entirely in the private sector. There has been a staggering rise of 30%—the highest since 1976—in the nationalized industries price index. Some part of this rise is due to more realistic pricing, in particular in the energy industries. But it also reflects the protected inefficiency of state industries.

The second encouraging sign is that, without benefit of formal incomes policy, unions and management began to settle for much lower wage increases from the Autumn of 1980 onward. British Leyland workers accepted 6.8% more; 2 million engineering workers settled for a rise of 8.2%; even the feared miners agreed to a formula giving them something around 12%—or about 3% below the year-on-year inflation rate. This modesty on pay is only one of several indications of greater economic realism on the shop-floor. The year 1980 also saw a reduction of two-thirds in the number of man-hours lost in strikes and industrial stoppages. Throughout industry, workers accepted lay-offs and redundancies in order to keep their factories in business.

Exports, too, have remained high despite the steady rise of the Pound. This has produced the most sustained series of balance of payments surpluses since 1971. One startling component of this success is Britain's trade with the rest of the European community. There was a visible trade surplus of $122 million with the EEC in 1980 as compared with a deficit of $7.2 billion in 1979.

It should finally be stressed that, despite the recession, real living standards in Britain reached what the *Economist* called "an all-time high in 1980," when prices rose by 16% and wages by 22%. Indeed, between 1977 and 1980, *real disposable income rose by an astonishing one-fifth.* Since real GDP rose only 1% over the period, this has its bad side; but it makes nonsense of such catastrophist assertions as those by Barbara Goodwin in *Dissent* (Winter 1981)—that Britain is characterized by a "stagnant economy and falling living standards" and that "the windfall of oil revenues only prevents living standards falling more rapidly." Nor is this rise in real incomes extracted unfairly from the unemployed and the old. Both pensions and unemployment payments have more than kept pace with inflation.

It is easier to recite these facts and figures than to explain them. One explanation has already been mentioned. It is that, despite appearances, the money supply has in fact been sharply reduced, leading to the classic first stage of monetary contraction in which production falls and unemployment rises. This has its optimistic side, however, because it also means that the fall in inflation, already begun, will continue for about another 2 years—and longer if this hypothetical monetary restraint is maintained.

It seems prudent, though, to consider the second explanation which at present is more generally accepted. This is that both the strengths and weaknesses of the British economy seem to result from the clash of a strong currency (itself the result of North Sea oil and high interest rates) and the high wage settlements of last year. The strong Pound, for instance, has lowered the price of imports and sharply increased the competitive stress on British companies. In order to retain their markets at home and abroad, they have in turn cut their prices, run down their stocks, and looked for every possible method of reducing their costs and improving productivity—a shakeout which will stand them in good stead when general economic conditions improve. In the present cold climate, however, this survivalism has been partly financed by a sharp drop in company profits. This income was, in effect, transferred to workers in the form of the high wage settlements of last year, and to consumers through the medium of prices kept low by competition. Hence, the rise in real disposable income and the rapid fall in the inflation rate.

On the other side of the coin, high wage settlements at a time of sticky prices, falling profits, and real competition led inevitably to higher unemployment. Workers literally priced themselves out of their jobs. And in the case of firms that were scarcely making a profit in the first place, they priced their companies out of business altogether and into bankruptcy. It should also be pointed out that the social benefits that make life more tolerable for the unemployed tend to increase the rate of unemployment. First, they are financed by what is, in effect, a tax, levied on each employed person and collected from the employer, which consequently makes labor more expensive. Recent increases in this tax to pay for increased benefits are responsible for part of the rise in unemployment. And, second, generous and effectively indexed benefits allow unemployed workers to be more choosy in selecting their next jobs, which necessarily adds to the rate of transitional unemployment.

But an important *caveat* should be entered here to qualify the general gloom. Economic statistics are likely to misleadingly dismal at present because of the growth in Britain of the "black" of underground economy. Sir William Pile, the head of the Inland Revenue, estimated last year the "unrecorded income" might be as high as 7.5% of the GNP. If the seemingly universal anecdotes about plumbers and electricians who offer a discount on bills paid in cash are accurate, then it may be even higher. This high level of economic activity outside the "official" economy would explain otherwise mysterious events, such as the record Christmas spending in supposedly distressed areas and the local conjunction of unfilled job vacancies and high rates of unemployment. One recent incident will illustrate the point. The Salvation Army recently opened a soup kitchen in a northern town with an official jobless rate of almost 20%. National newspapers on the following morning showed the two volunteer workers drinking their own soup after entertaining only one unemployed visitor during the entire day.

Certain obvious conclusions follow. Unemployment figures would clearly exaggerate the severity of joblessness. National income figures would understate real income. So would figures for production understate the reality. Retail price figures would almost certainly be too high since cash payments for underground goods and services are at a discount almost by definition. Even high money supply figures would not be so worrisome since the money would in part be going to finance underground transactions rather than simply fueling inflation. We can speculate further. If the underground economy grows faster than the official economy in conditions of high and rising taxation, as seems likely, then a given rate of increase in the quantity of money is likely to stimulate a slower rate of inflation than might otherwise be expected. That might be part of the explanation for the present lower-than-expected inflation.

We, therefore, have reasonable grounds for qualified optimism about the "Thatcher experiment." At the end of 1980, *Incomes Data* estimated that wage settlements were running between 2.5 and 4% "below the perceived rate of inflation." As inflation continues its predicted fall throughout this year, and as perceptions catch up with this reality, wage settlements are likely to follow it downward. Indeed, this is already happening. After a time-lag, this will, in turn, first reduce and then reverse the rise in unemployment. Workers will start pricing themselves *into* jobs. In short, there is the possibility in these circumstances of a "virtuous circle" in which lower inflation leads to lower money wage settlements which in turn lead to greater employment and higher real output.

Slightly favorable though these signs are, however, they principally effect the secondary and recent British disease of high inflation. These are gloomier portents about the more profound malaise of low growth and persistent inefficiency. Admittedly, the recession, with its threat of bankruptcies, has wrought important attitude changes on the shop floor, notably a willingness to adopt more efficient working methods, which in turn have led to improvements in productivity. But will these new attitudes survive the return of full-time working and increased demand for labor? It was during this respite, surely, that legislative and institutional changes ought to have been introduced. But trade union power remains legally unconstrained; scarce investible resources continue to be misallocated by government, indeed, on a scale larger than ever; marginal tax rates, though reduced, are still high by international standards; and the public sector is as large and wastefully inefficient as ever. The British disease seems likely to persist, therefore, for quite some time to come. And Thatcherism will be said to have failed. But will it have been tried?

CHAPTER 6

An Overview of Government Regulation

MURRAY L. WEIDENBAUM

In any discussion of the relationship between government and business, it is useful to recognize that this is an area in which there is very little perceived or received "truth." There are simply a host of value judgments supported by a very small and frequently contradictory set of "facts." My value judgments should come as no surprise to those of you who have read anything that I have written. I am certainly not of the school of thought that believes that business should rend its garments, don sackcloth and ashes, and recite from the *Book of Lamentations* (or *Unsafe at Any Speed*). If anything, I think we as a society have been far too swift in delivering blanket condemnations of the business sector.

Like anyone who has ever breathed dirty air or drunk contaminated water, I am concerned about what our business sector does to the society. However, as a purchaser of goods and services, I am also concerned about what business firms do for us as consumers. I see the business system as performing a "middleman" function between producers and consumers. Private firms

The Limits of Government Regulation

ISBN 0-12-277620-8 0-12-277622-4(p)

provide the jobs that enable us to purchase the goods and services that they produce in response to our demands.

I do not want to dwell on this point, but I find it fascinating that this function is so completely ignored by the more vocal critics of the business community. The latest example was April 17, Big Business Day. I do not think that it is a day that will live in infamy; I do not think that it will live much beyond April 17. But I do think that this event exemplifies the nature of the adverse criticism, in that from listening to its sponsors, we gather that they apparently find in our private, free market economy no positive aspect that is worthy of mention. This group views the amelioration of society's ills as the central function of the business sector and judges its performance on that basis. Their long recitation of the social obligations of the firm totally ignores its central role of satisfying consumer demands, creating jobs and income, and producing goods and services.

The demands of these so-called corporate activists have resulted in the largest, most rapid increase in regulatory controls and governmental agencies that our nation has ever experienced. In the past 20 years, we have seen a proliferation of government intervention in the private sector that dwarfs even the experience of the 1930s. I have tallied up some 57 agencies that have been established to deal with job safety, environmental protection, product safety, discrimination, pensions, etc. A simple listing, which excludes a description of the laws that provide the multiple mandates for these agencies, requires a sizable chapter in a standard textbook.

However, it is not the sheer number of these agencies that concerns me, but rather their impact on the ability of the business sector to perform its central function. If you look at the modern regulatory phenomenon from the viewpoint of the typical firm, the nature of the problem becomes apparent. Let us consider the president of some hypothetical company. He or she will typically oversee a number of departments, such as personnel, finance, research and development, etc., which handle a variety of tasks required for the efficient operation of the company. You will find that for every box on the organizational chart, there are one or more government agencies heavily involved in the company's internal decision making. From the perspective of this firm, the impact is in one direction: to increase the overhead and operating costs, and to reduce the resources available to perform its major task of producing goods and services for the consumer. To the economist, this is part of the "opportunity cost" of government regulation.

I have not mentioned, of course, the benefits of added regulation—and to the extent that we have cleaner air, cleaner water, and so forth, these benefits exist. The question, however, is whether the benefits of the increased regulation are worth the added costs. From the viewpoint of the consumer, the bottom line is not the impact on the government or the business system but the impact on the consumer.

The most measurable, but possibly least important cost is the increase in the price of goods and services. This is only one thing among many contributing to a higher rate of inflation. Very frankly, if that were the only factor involved, you might find the added regulation worth the cost. However, when one goes beyond the dollar signs to less easily quantified impacts, other more subtle and more serious costs emerge. Central among these is research and development, one of the many functions affected by regulation. By and large, regulation has tended to reduce the flow of innovations, of new and better products, because we have a variety of government regulatory agencies with the power—which they have frequently exercised—of deciding whether or not a new product will go on the market.

Ostensibly, the justification for this power is that it keeps off the market unsafe or ineffective products. Unfortunately the reality is often quite different. Let me give you an example. If you look at mortality data, you find that for decades the number one cause of death in this country has not been cancer, but cardiovascular disease—heart attacks and strokes. There is a series of new drugs called beta blockers which are in widespread use in the United Kingdom and other developed nations. In the United

States, however, introduction of these drugs has been stalled by the Food and Drug Administration (FDA). According to the research of Professor William Wardell at the University of Rochester Medical School, one of these beta blockers, practolol, which is currently in widespread use in Western Europe, would save 10,000 lives a year if introduced in the United States. And beta blockers are not the only drugs kept out of the U.S. market by the FDA. Professor Wardell has examined the list of drugs newly approved by the FDA. In case after case, the United States was one of the last countries—32nd, 58th, 140th, etc.—to accept many other drugs in this long list.

This is not surprising given the cardinal rule for bureaucratic survival: Do not stick your neck out. If you were an FDA review officer and you were to approve practolol, you would be taking a risk. If anybody suffers an adverse reaction, you will quite possibly bear the responsibility. On the other hand, if you do not approve the drug, the potential users are unlikely to complain, since they are unlikely to know about it. As a result, you do not say no—you simply ask for more studies; you delay.

Another area in which business firms find the heavy hand of regulation increasingly present is product safety. The Consumer Product Safety Commission (CPSC) has the authority to order companies to engage in "reverse distribution." For the layman, that is product recall. Again, no one objects to safe products, but bureaucratic incentives too often have resulted in ridiculous actions whose consequences can be tragic. One example is CPSC's action with regard to aerosol spray adhesives, an art supply product. An academic researcher had done research that indicated that pregnant women who had used these sprays had higher probabilities of bearing children with birth defects. He submitted his findings to the CPSC, which in turn contacted the producers for their response. The relevant companies requested a copy of the agency's report but were only allowed to see excerpts. They questioned the validity of the study based on what they had seen, but agreed to recall the aerosol adhesives.

An official ban was issued; the sprays were recalled. Then the

CPSC did something that is commendable but unfortunately very unusual. It began a full-scale review of the problem to see whether the first study was accurate. It was not, and the ban was lifted. All this was done in a period of 7 months—which must have set a speed record for a government agency. On the face of it, the CPSC's action was commendable. It publicly admitted its error and reversed its decision. Consumers were deprived of this spray for only 7 months, which is a small price to pay for safe products—or so it *seemed.*

You see, there is an O'Henry twist to the story. During the 7-month period a number of pregnant women who had used the spray read of the reason for the ban and underwent abortions solely because they did not want to incur the risk of deformed children. There are nine documented cases. Unfortunately, although the CPSC decision was reversible, the abortions were not.

The frightening thing about this case is that there really are no villains. Everyone was attempting to do the correct thing as he or she saw it, but everyone from the researcher to the CPSC administrator underestimated the power of the official announcement and failed to consider the full range of the consequences of their actions.

A less dramatic, but nonetheless powerful, indictment of regulatory action is the case of the Occupational Safety and Health Administration (OSHA). If you look at the Department of Labor's own data on days lost per worker due to job-related illness or accident, you find that the ratio has not declined since OSHA began to operate—this despite the billions of dollars in extra costs that the agency imposes on industry. That, to me, suggests that there are no net benefits from OSHA and that its regulations are imposing a "dead weight" loss on society. On the other hand, if we were seeing a significant reduction in workplace injury and, hence, a more productive work force, that would suggest regulation that more than pays for itself.

I do not think this issue involves a philosophical question such as, Are you for or against government intervention? It involves a very practical one: Does this specific type of government intervention work? The sad reality is that, as often as not, it does not. This reality has been recognized in some areas, but not in others. On the one hand, deregulating airlines has benefited the traveling public as well as the airlines and the employees, and I think deregulating the trucking industry will do the same. But on the other hand, in the case of environmental regulation, every economic study I have ever seen has shown that there is another way of accomplishing the goals that would result in at least the same amount of additional clear air or water at a small fraction of the current costs. That other way involves working through the price system by means of some combination of pollution taxes or pollution permits. Belatedly, economists are gaining support for that position from environmentalists such as the Friends of the Earth and the Sierra Club. Unfortunately, businesses still take an adamantly negative position. They do not want regulation, but if there must be regulation, they want the most inefficient regulation so they can gripe about it and try to delay it in court.

This is not, of course, a basis for eliminating government regulation. It does demonstrate, however, that government intervention is a very powerful but extremely imperfect tool. You must use it very carefully, with full awareness of all side effects. Certainly there are problems in society, and certainly government regulatory activities generate some benefits. So the serious concern here is to balance the benefits that are likely to result against the various costs and side effects associated with regulatory actions.

In this regard, the public debate tends to constitute a stacked deck. Those bearing the banner of "public interest" groups are automatically treated by the media as the good guys in the white hats. If you disagree with their position, it is assumed that you are the villainous "heavy" unconcerned with the public's welfare. But the last time I checked, "public interest" advocates were mortal human beings and thus had less than perfect knowledge.

These advocates also have their own agendas. If you look at the results of public opinion polls on the problems facing this nation, you will find that inflation is ranked number one and unemployment number two. Yet, the proposals of the so-called corporate activists and "public interest" outfits generate simultaneously (and perhaps unwillingly) more inflation and more unemployment. If their banner is accurate, their methods are self-defeating.

A while ago I was at a conference with Ralph Nader. I attended the session at which he spoke. The talk he gave consisted of an attack, a very personal attack, on the business community. When he finished an hour or more later, the chairman asked for questions. I was amazed. Not one of the business representatives had the gumption to question him. (What that says about the business sector is not very flattering.) Well, I could not resist, and I said, "Mr. Nader, you are a leading consumer advocate, and every poll shows inflation is the number one problem on the minds of Americans. Why is it, then, that not once during your speech did you mention inflation? In fact some of your proposals would only worsen the inflationary problem."

I was not prepared for the response. He said, "Inflation is only an academic question; the people don't really care." If I may interpret that answer, it says, "I, Ralph Nader, do not think inflation is an important question, and therefore, the people should not care."

I do not claim to represent the public interest. I have spent many years in government, helping to make government policy, and I have never met a mortal man or woman who represented *the* public interest. In fact, good government policy, if you ever get it, reconciles a variety of bona fide, legitimate interests. Is clean air a legitimate interest? Of course it is. Is high employment legitimate? Is bringing down inflation legitimate? Is producing safer products legitimate? The answer to each of these questions is yes. They are all legitimate interests. However, until we have a mechanism for balancing these legitimate interests with their costs—rather than taking the simple-minded approach of labeling one set of interests, public interests, which are good, and labeling the other set special or business interests, which are presumably bad—we are going to continue to have high inflation accompanied by high unemployment. In short, we must discard the activist notion that simply because an action may possibly generate some benefit, it is good. Similarly, the business community must stop taking the stance that any regulation that generates high costs is bad.

Unfortunately, the rapid growth of regulation has not ended, and it is not about to end soon. If you look into the pipeline of regulation, you will see that a host of statutes passed in the late 1970s are still generating regulations whose costs will not hit us until the 1980s. For example, there is TOSCA. To opera buffs, that is a melodrama that ends in tragedy. To the chemical industry, it is the Toxic Substances Control Act. (There may be a parallel there.) There are also the Resource Conservation and Recovery Act and the Clean Air and Clean Water Amendments of 1977, to name just a few. So although we have seen some moves toward deregulation, it has been a matter of one step forward and three steps backward. At the same time the Carter administration deregulated the airlines and OSHA eliminated the so-called "Mickey Mouse" regulations (i.e., those concerning such questions as: When is a roof a floor? How big is a hole? How often must a spittoon be cleaned?), OSHA established the Generic Carcenogenic Standard, which is likely to generate more compliance costs than all existing OSHA standards put together.

In a capsule, if Big Business Day has been generated as a way of developing public support for yet another round of government control over the American corporation, my response, echoing phraseology from earlier days, is simple: Free the Fortune 500.

CHAPTER 7

Cost of Government Regulation Study[1]

THE BUSINESS ROUNDTABLE
ARTHUR ANDERSEN & CO.

STIMULUS FOR THE STUDY

The mid 1960s and early 1970s brought significant additions to traditional federal regulatory objectives. The additional objectives were to achieve desirable social goals—cleaner air, safer and healthier working conditions, equal employment opportunities for all—through federal regulation. New regulatory agencies were formed whose impacts extended across industry lines. As the agencies became more numerous and took on additional regulatory functions, and as their budgets grew larger, they issued and continue to issue increasing numbers of regulations—detailed rules which often prescribe specific behavior. Business has been confronted with a vast array of regulatory constraints that stipulate how to conduct operating activities.

As regulation has increased, so has the concern about the

[1] This chapter is adapted from *Cost of Government Regulation Study*, published by The Business Roundtable, March 1979.

ISBN 0-12-277620-8 0-12-277622-4(p)

regulatory process and its effects. Some of the concern reflects a growing awareness that the costs of regulation to the nation are substantial and a growing fear that in many instances the costs of particular regulations may outweigh their benefits. Some believe that even if new regulation passes a cost-benefit test, there is a limit to the amount of regulation the economy can absorb at a given time, and that priorities need to be established. The concerns result at least in part from a perception that many regulations are enacted without adequate evaluation of their economic impact on the nation.

The Business Roundtable believes that some government intervention in the economy is necessary to achieve desirable social goals and that, in many instances, specific regulations are well conceived and implemented. However, it also holds that the proposed form of government intervention requires more careful analysis prior to adoption to ensure that the stated goals are both attainable and worth the additional cost to the economy required to achieve them, and that the proposed form of intervention—the particular regulation—is the best and most efficient way of achieving the goal.

Early in 1978, The Business Roundtable initiated a cost of government regulation study to determine the cost of complying with the regulations of selected federal agencies. The Business Roundtable retained Arthur Andersen & Co. to design a cost determination methodology and then conduct the study.

The study was commissioned in the belief that regulatory policymakers at all levels of government need more useful data pertaining to the benefits and costs of specific regulatory measures. The Business Roundtable recognized that there is little in the accounting and engineering records of companies that would measure the social benefits of regulations. Those same records, however, are a unique source of valuable information regarding the incremental costs of regulation.

Although the focus of this study was on incremental costs, The Business Roundtable fully recognized that an assessment of benefits and less visible costs is equally important in making final judgments regarding the effectiveness of any particular regulatory measure. By developing a standard methodology to collect and report specific details regarding the incremental cost of complying with regulations, the study was intended to provide a credible contribution to the base of knowledge needed by those interested in improving the regulatory process.

OVERVIEW OF THE STUDY AND METHODOLOGY

The Business Roundtable cost of government regulation study was designed to provide more specific information than previous cost studies by identifying high cost regulations and by seeking to identify the attributes that characterize them. Accordingly, one of the major objectives of the study was to develop a comprehensive methodology to determine by accounting methods the incremental costs of compliance with specific regulations for a large number of companies and industries, to identify the high cost and problem regulations, and to report observations and recommendations made by participating companies.

The six regulatory agencies[2] selected for study were:

1. Environmental Protection Agency (EPA)
2. Equal Employment Opportunity (EEO)
3. Occupational Safety and Health Administration (OSHA)
4. Department of Energy (DOE)
5. Employee Retirement Income Security Act (ERISA)
6. Federal Trade Commission (FTC)

The agencies were selected on the basis that they were perceived to have a significant cost impact on a broad cross-section of Business Roundtable member companies and industries. Furthermore, the cost impact of these agencies was expected to increase through future regulatory programs.

Forty-eight member companies of The Business Roundtable (Figure 7.1) elected to participate in the study. Not all companies

[2] The term *agency* is applied throughout the study to each of these six regulatory areas. Only designated portions of DOE and FTC were included in the study.

Allied Chemical Corporation
American Telephone & Telegraph Company
Atlantic Richfield Company
Bethlehem Steel Corporation
Carolina Power & Light Company
Champion International Corporation
Chase Manhattan Bank N.A.
Citicorp
Continental Illinois Corporation
Crown Zellerbach Corporation
The Dow Chemical Company
Dresser Industries, Inc.
E.I. du Pont de Nemours & Company
Eastman Kodak Company
Eaton Corporation
Exxon Corporation
General Electric Company
General Foods Corporation
General Motors Corporation
Georgia-Pacific Corporation
The Goodyear Tire & Rubber Company
Gulf Oil Corporation
Hoover Worldwide Corporation
Illinois Tool Works Inc.
Inland Steel Company
International Business Machines Corporation
Kraft, Inc.
Eli Lilly & Company
Mobil Oil Corporation
Monsanto Company
National Steel Corporation
Owens-Corning Fiberglas Corporation
Phillips Petroleum Company
Potomac Electric Power Company
PPG Industries, Inc.
The Procter & Gamble Company
Roadway Express, Inc.
Shell Oil Company
SmithKline Corporation
Southern California Gas Company
Stauffer Chemical Company
TRW Inc.
Texaco, Inc.
Texasgulf Inc.
Union Pacific Corporation
Western Electric Company, Inc.
Westinghouse Electric Corporation
Whirlpool Corporation

Figure 7.1. The 48 companies participating in the study.

included all of their domestic operations in the study of each agency. For example, in the oil and gas industry, seven companies studied EPA and OSHA for only portions of their business operations.

The significance of the 48 participating companies in the U.S. economy is illustrated in Figure 7.2 which displays the companies' shares of the U.S. civilian labor force excluding agriculture and government workers, sales of certain industrial sectors, and capital investment.

The study measured the incremental costs incurred in 1977 by participating companies to comply with regulations of the six agencies. Incremental cost in this study is the cost of an action taken to comply with a regulation that would not have been taken in the absence of that regulation. Figure 7.3 illustrates how incremental cost was calculated.

The incremental cost determination required each company to apply its best judgment to decide which actions it would have taken in the absence of regulation. The introduction of judgment

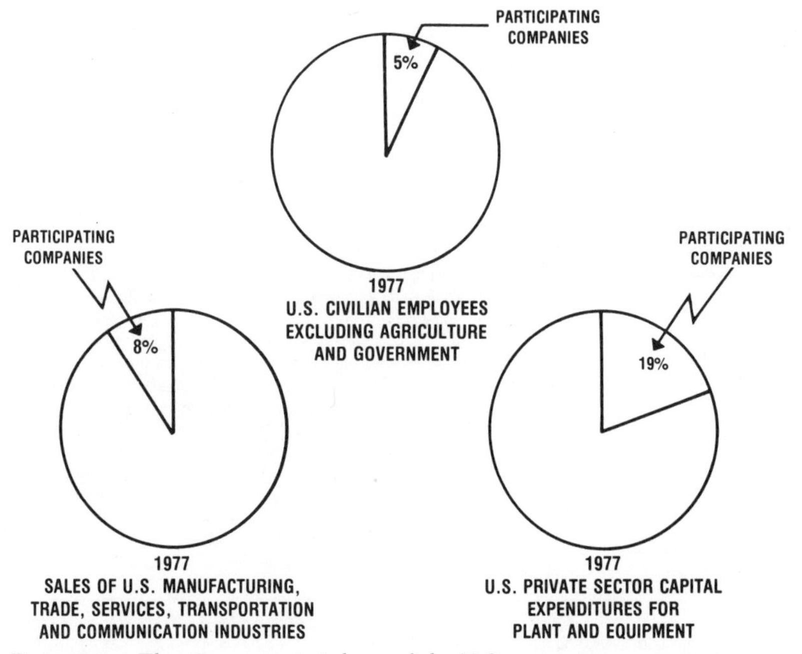

Figure 7.2. The 48 companies' share of the U.S. economy.

into the calculation of incremental cost has been questioned by some. However, different companies do indeed make different judgments as to which actions to take in the absence of regulation. By requiring that judgment, the study was able to measure costs incurred to comply with regulations that would have been applied to other purposes in the absence of regulations. Arthur Andersen & Co. believes the focus on incremental cost to be a strength of the study.

The Business Roundtable cost of government regulation study represents the first attempt to measure the incremental costs of regulation with a methodology applied consistently across federal agency and industry lines. It is important to recognize the areas defined as outside the scope of the study.

The Business Roundtable understands that regulation is an important element in our economic system and provides many useful

	Steps to Take in Computing Incremental Cost	Example Illustrating Methodology
1.	Company identifies actions taken in 1977 to comply with a specific regulation of one of the six agencies.	In building a new plant in 1977, Company A installed a system to pretreat waste water before discharging it into the county's sewer system where it would be treated again. The action was taken to comply with the provisions of EPA's water pretreatment standards (Title 40 CFR, Chapter 1, Part 128).
2.	Company determines whether it would have taken action in the absence of regulation.	The new pretreatment system was designed to remove 99% of the incompatible pollutants from the waste water introduced into the county's treatment works. Pretreatment systems used by the company at similar facilities prior to the new regulation were designed to remove 95% of the incompatible pollutants. Company A determined that, had it not been for the regulation requiring the removal of 99% of the incompatible pollutants, it would have installed a system similar to the systems at other plants. In its opinion, based on scientific research and studies, introducing 5% of the incompatible pollutants into the county's treatment works would result in no measurable damage to the county's system and no detrimental effects downstream. Since the company determined that the regulation resulted in an action beyond what it would have taken in the absence of regulation, the company went to the next step of determining the cost of the action.
3.	Company determines cost of action through reference to accounting or other records.	Referring to its fixed asset ledger, Company A identified the cost of installing the new pretreatment system to be \$1,200,000.
4.	Company determines the cost of the action that would have been taken in absence of regulation and the cost of that action.	Referring to previous years' fixed asset ledgers, engineering studies and the current cost of construction, Company A determined that the cost of installing a pretreatment system similar to those that had been used throughout the company (i.e., removing 95% of the incompatible pollutants) would have been \$800,000 in 1977.
5.	Company calculates incremental cost by subtracting the cost of the action it would have taken in the absence of regulation (4) from the cost of the action it did take (3).	Company A's incremental cost was \$400,000 (\$1,200,000 less \$800,000). The \$400,000 would be classified as an incremental capital cost of regulation in 1977.

Figure 7.3. Calculation of incremental cost.

benefits to all Americans. However, benefits are often difficult to measure. They are usually evaluated on a community-wide basis and cannot be based solely upon the accounting and engineering records of business firms.

The data collected in this study are, by contrast, uniquely

determinable from the business records of companies. For the first time, these data provide a snapshot of the incremental cost impact of regulation on an important segment of the business community in one year—1977.

As stressed earlier, incremental costs of regulation did not include costs that the company decided it would have incurred anyway. For example, EEO requires affirmative action programs which in turn call for special recruiting and training, for scholarships, internships, and related programs, and for facilities for the benefit of minorities, women, and handicapped persons. Many of the costs for these actions can be attributed to the regulations and, hence, could be considered part of the total cost of regulation. However, most companies considered many of the actions to be ones they would have taken in 1977 even in the absence of regulation. In those cases, they excluded the costs from the incremental costs of regulation.

In addition to incremental costs of regulation, there are many less visible secondary effects that cause substantial costs to the companies and to society generally. Some companies collected information about secondary effects of regulation and the costs associated with them, but those costs were excluded from the incremental cost calculation.

Three examples of secondary effects excluded from incremental costs are:

1. Opportunity costs
2. Changes in productivity
3. Costs of regulatory-caused delays

Companies pointed out that these costs often exceeded the incremental cost of compliance. For example, regulatory-caused delays in constructing the Trans-Alaska pipeline and in bringing off-shore wells into production had a detrimental impact on jobs, supplies of petroleum, and the balance of payments. Excluded from incremental costs were hundreds of millions of dollars for opportunity costs on invested capital.

The costs of secondary effects are much more difficult to

measure than incremental costs as defined. Therefore, it was decided to exclude them from incremental costs because they could not be measured with reasonable precision from available accounting and engineering records. Figure 7.4 illustrates the conceptual relationship of incremental costs and the costs of secondary effects.

The six federal agencies chosen for study account for only a part of the regulatory impact that is imposed by all federal agencies with regulatory functions and by the regulations of state and local governments.

All industry-specific agencies were excluded from the study, as the principal focus was on agencies having a cross-industry impact. Although the automobile industry was represented in the study, the costs imposed by regulations of the National Highway Traffic Safety Administration were excluded; although the drug industry participated, the Food and Drug Administration was excluded; although the communications industry was in the study,

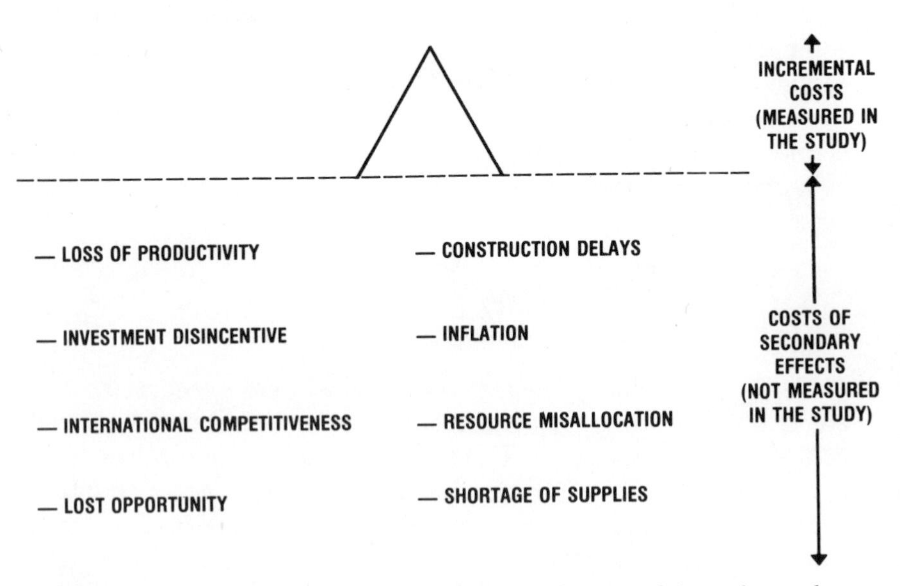

Figure 7.4. Conceptual relationship of incremental costs and costs of secondary effects.

the costs associated with the Federal Communications Commission were not counted; and although the banking industry participated, the costs for the Comptroller of the Currency's regulations were not included.

Although this was a cross-industry study, certain major industries and many large companies were not represented given that the study was confined to a volunteer group of Business Roundtable member companies. No small businesses were included.[3]

The major industries not represented were agriculture, airline transportation, construction, insurance, printing and publishing, retailing, textile and apparel manufacturing, real estate, the majority of service industries, and state and local government.

Several industries that reported substantial incremental costs—such as primary metals, fabricated metals, food and kindred products, electric and gas services, and others—were represented by only a small number of companies.

OVERVIEW OF THE STUDY RESULTS

The 48 participating companies reported $2.6 billion of incremental costs in 1977 in complying with regulations of the six federal agencies and programs under study. Some of the significance of that amount can be illustrated by comparing it to selected 1977 financial data for those companies as shown in Figure 7.5.

The manufacturing sector was impacted most heavily; manufacturing companies incurred $2.3 billion of the incremental costs. A comparison of incremental costs with selected 1977 financial data for the manufacturing sector is shown in Figure 7.6.

The comparison of incremental costs of regulation with selected

[3] Arthur Andersen & Co. has announced a similar study of the costs of regulation of smaller businesses to provide information that will complement The Business Roundtable study data base.

Total capital expenditures	$25.8 billion
Total research and development costs	$ 6.0 billion
Net income after taxes	$16.6 billion
Incremental costs of regulations (6 agencies)	$ 2.6 billion

Figure 7.5. Comparison of incremental cost to selected financial data for all participating companies.

Total capital expenditures	$13.4 billion
Total research and development costs	$ 5.4 billion
Net income after taxes	$10.2 billion
Incremental costs of regulations (6 agencies)	$ 2.3 billion

Figure 7.6. Comparison of incremental cost to selected financial data for participating manufacturing companies.

financial data in Figures 7.5 and 7.6 is not intended to imply that, had they not been expended for regulatory costs, all of the incremental costs would necessarily have been applied to capital expenditures or research and development, or that they would have resulted in additional net income or dividends.

The $2.6 billion of incremental costs was identified with four specified classifications: capital, operating and administrative, research and development, and product. Figure 7.7 shows how this amount is distributed among the four cost classifications.

Passed on in the form of price increases, $2.6 billion of incremental costs would have an average of 1.1% price level impact for the participating companies. The $2.3 billion incurred by manufacturing companies would have an average of 1.4% price level impact for the manufacturing companies. This adds to inflationary pressures and adversely affects U.S. industry's ability to compete in domestic and foreign markets.

Of the $2.6 billion total, $870 million of incremental capital costs was incurred in 1977 to comply with regulations of the six agencies. This is equivalent to 3.3% of the total capital expenditures of the participating companies in 1977 for those operations included in the study. The $803 million of incremental capital costs incurred by the manufacturing companies is equivalent to

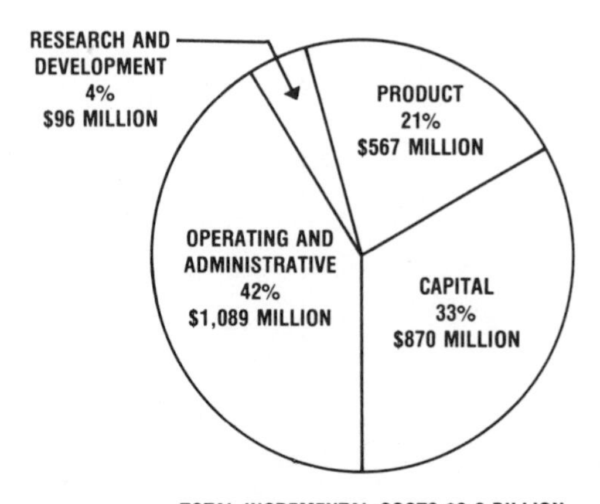

Figure 7.7. Incremental costs summarized in four classifications.

more than 6% of the total capital expenditures of their operations included in the study.

Of incremental capital costs, $1.6 billion was incurred prior to 1977, and an estimated $1.4 billion will be incurred after 1977 to complete capital projects active in 1977, bringing the total incremental capital costs of those projects to $3.9 billion.

In addition to capital costs, capital projects active in 1977 are expected to add $305 million in recurring annual incremental operating costs. That amount does not include depreciation.

Of incremental operating and administrative and research and development costs, $1.2 billion were incurred in 1977. The operating and administrative costs are annual costs and consequently represent a recurring annual impact on prices. Figure 7.8 shows the distribution between labor and nonlabor costs.

A total of $532 million of incremental labor costs were incurred in 1977 by the 41 companies that segregated costs between labor and nonlabor sources. This amount represents an average incremental labor cost of $164 per employee for these companies, an addition of nearly 1% to the average wage cost, including fringe benefits.

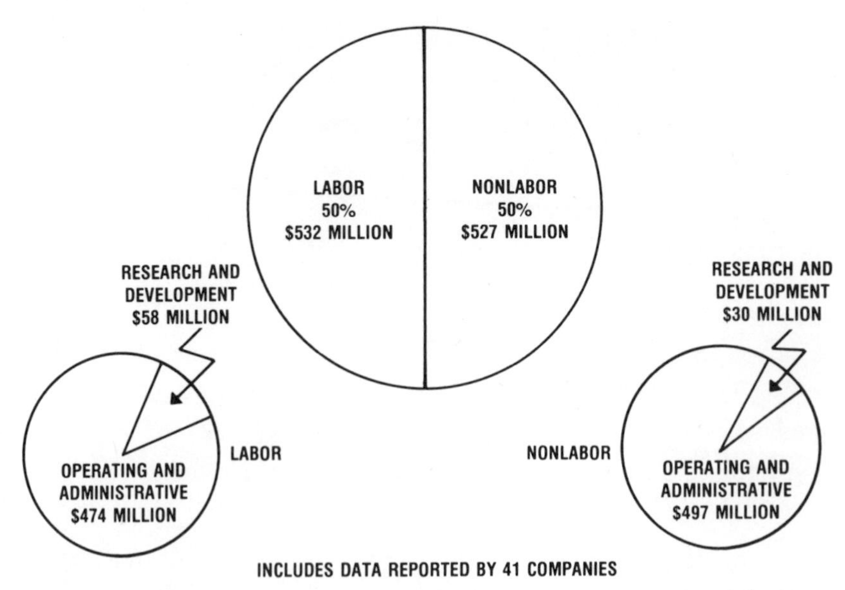

Figure 7.8. Analysis of operating and administrative, and research and development cost sources.

The additional paperwork burden imposed by these agencies on the participating companies involved the completion of more than 5 million pages.

As stated earlier, the costs of secondary effects were excluded from incremental costs. However, many companies reported instances where the costs of secondary effects were even higher than incremental costs. For example:

- Several companies reported significant delays in construction of new plants and equipment due to regulatory restrictions. Frequently, the delays occurred after the projects had begun and after millions of dollars had been invested. In some instances the delays amounted to many years.
- Certain regulations encourage the increased use of oil, and others encourage the use of low sulfur oil. As the demand for oil, particularly low sulfur oil, has not been satisfied by domestic production, the result is to increase reliance on

foreign oil and affect the U.S. balance of payments adversely.

Many companies reported that where regulations prescribe the specific method by which regulatory goals must be achieved, there was often an adverse effect on productivity of both equipment and labor. Companies reported that they could have achieved the goals in a more cost-effective manner had they been given the latitude to do so. For example, companies do not agree with OSHA's insistence upon feasible engineering controls to control worker exposure to noise, when they believe that personal protective equipment would be just as effective at far less cost.

The complexity and rate of change of many regulations has caused companies to spend a considerable amount of executive and managerial resources to comply with existing regulations and to keep current with new and revised regulations.

Incremental costs vary considerably among the six agencies. Figure 7.9 shows incremental costs for each agency.

Analysis of regulations in the study and compliance actions taken by companies indicates that regulations with high incremen-

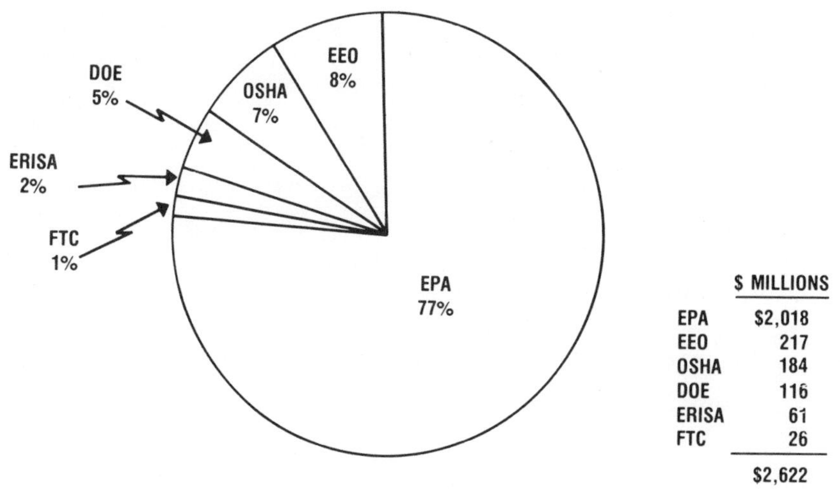

Figure 7.9. Incremental costs by agency

tal costs are usually associated with certain attributes. Conversely, the absence of these attributes tends to be a characteristic of regulations with lower compliance costs. If the attributes are proven to be reliable indicators of high cost regulations, they may be used to predict which proposed regulations will be most likely to have a high incremental cost impact on the industries affected. In that way, the economic impact studies for the potentially costly regulations may be performed with greater care. Some of the more important attributes identified in the course of the study are shown in Figure 7.10.

This is not necessarily an exhaustive list of all of the attributes of all high cost regulations; however, it does represent a comprehensive list of the types of attributes that were associated with high incremental costs for the regulations included in this study. Arthur Andersen & Co. believes this list of attributes may be useful to business and regulators in identifying proposed regulations with potentially high cost. The presence of one or more of the attributes in proposed regulations or legislation should provide a predictive capability in making that identification.

A number of estimates have been made of the costs to the private sector of government regulations. Some estimates have included all levels of government, all businesses in the United States, and both economic and social costs. Others have focused on individual areas of regulation, selected types of cost and specific industries. For example:

- Murray L. Weidenbaum and Robert De Fina of the Center for Study of American Business at Washington University estimated the total cost of federal regulation in 1977 to be $79.1 billion. Roughly $9.5 billion of this was attributed to environmental regulations. Their estimate was based in part on estimates provided by several industry and agency specific studies conducted by others.
- The Office of Management and Budget (OMB) estimated the 1975 total costs of regulation to be in the range of $113.3–$135.4 billion. The General Accounting Office's

1.	Continuous Monitoring	Requires evidence of compliance by means of round-the-clock monitoring devices or continuous maintenance of comprehensive records of actions taken and results achieved.
2.	Forcing New Technology	Requirements to meet a level of compliance not achievable with available technology, often effected through legislation or regulations specifying a deadline for meeting a stringent standard or the specific requirement to use advanced technology.
3.	Capital Intensity	Requires the purchase of new equipment or modification of existing equipment.
4.	Recurring Costs	Requires actions which lead to continuing costs of operation or maintenance.
5.	Retrofitting	Requires modification of existing facilities, not just application to new facilities.
6.	Specified Compliance Action	Requires a specified method of compliance without flexibility to recognize differing circumstances for application of alternate techniques to achieve the desired objective.
7.	Inadequate Risk Assessment	Requires compliance with a stringent standard even though the risks have not been adequately assessed.
8.	Engineering Solutions	Requires the elimination of a hazardous substance or condition by engineering methods rather than specific mechanical protection of endangered workers or other individuals.
9.	Changing Requirements	Requires adaptation to rules which are frequently changed or are subject to delay in being defined, during which time capital spending plans must be made without knowledge of compliance requirements which will be imposed.

Figure 7.10. Attributes of regulations with high incremental costs.

(GAO) economic evaluation of OMB's study concluded that OMB's estimate was significantly overstated, but did not establish an alternate estimate.

- Edward F. Denison of the Brookings Institution estimated the incremental costs to protect the environment and the safety and health of workers in 1975 was $10.5 billion, $9.5 billion of which was attributed to environmental regulations. He also estimated that in 1975 these factors resulted in a .5% annual reduction in growth of output of net national product per unit of input. Denison's method of calculating incremental cost was substantially different from that used in The Business Roundtable study.
- The Council on Environmental Quality (CEQ) study estimated the incremental cost for all businesses to comply with pollution abatement control requirements in 1977 to be $12.8 billion. The CEQ's method of calculating incremental cost was also different from that used in The Business Roundtable study.

The foregoing studies each made important contributions to the public's awareness that the costs of regulation to our economy and to our society are very high.

The Business Roundtable study's major objective—to provide specific data that will contribute to improving the regulatory process—dictated a study with a different scope. It was concerned with identifying the costs of a specific group of regulations, not the total cost of regulations. The Business Roundtable study's results nonetheless are not inconsistent with earlier studies in concluding that the cost of regulation is high.

ENVIRONMENTAL PROTECTION AGENCY

Environmental Protection Agency (EPA) regulations account for more than $2 billion, 77% of the total incremental costs for the six agencies. The incremental costs represent only a portion of the incremental costs imposed by environmental regulations on the companies, because the regulatory requirements of the Bureau of Land Management, and national preservation laws and other environmental regulations, were not included. Furthermore, EPA costs collected by seven oil and gas companies apply to only a part of their operations and, consequently, only a portion of their regulatory costs are represented. Figure 7.11, the analysis of the four classifications of EPA costs, shows that incremental capital and product costs were very high in 1977, as were recurring annual operating and administrative costs.

In many cases incremental capital expenditures incurred during 1977 were associated with projects that were long term in nature, as shown in Figure 7.12.

The total incremental cost of these projects is four times the portion incurred in 1977, and recurring annual operating expenses associated with them are estimated to be over $257 million. These costs relate only to capital projects in progress during the study year and do not include significant amounts for projects fore-

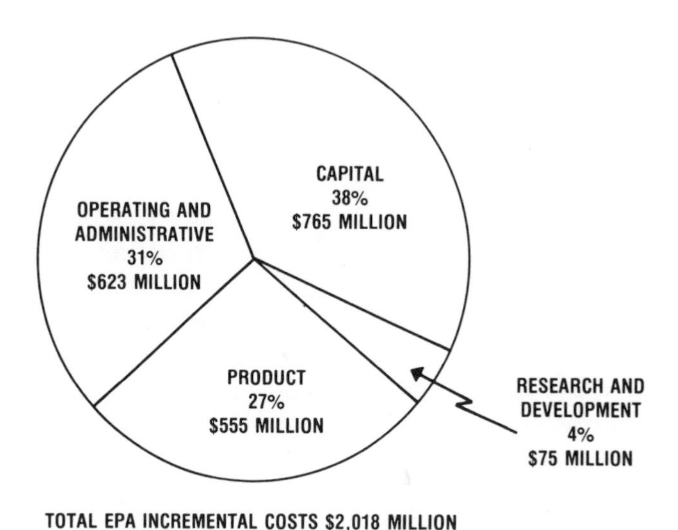

Figure 7.11. EPA incremental costs summarized in four classifications.

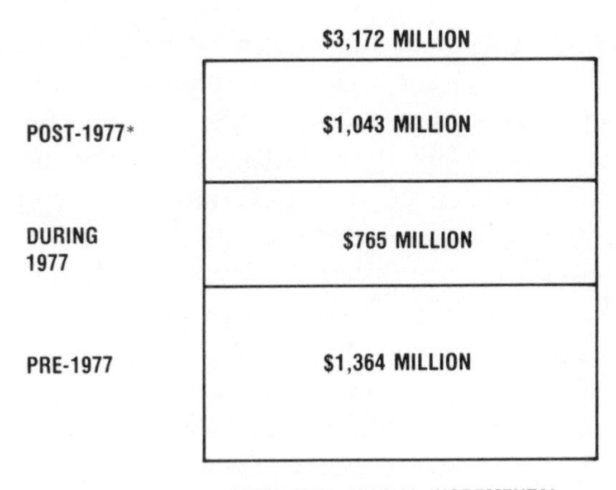

Figure 7.12. EPA incremental costs of 1977 projects in progress.

casted, but not started, at the end of 1977, or for projects completed prior to 1977.

For five industries, the 1977 incremental capital costs represented more than 9% of their total capital expenditures in 1977. These industries were electricity and gas services, primary metals, chemicals and allied products, paper and allied products, and lumber and wood.

One of the objectives of the study was to demonstrate the disparate effect of each agency on individual industries. With respect to EPA regulations, the four industries that emerged with the highest incremental cost impact relative to their share of the sales, capital expenditures, and number of employees were the following: The electric and gas services industry, with only 1.4% of the sales of participating companies, accounted for 4.4% of incremental costs incurred by all participating companies; the chemicals and allied products industry accounted for 11% of sales and incurred 28% of incremental costs; the primary metals industry accounted for 4% of sales and 11% of incremental costs;

and, finally, the transportation equipment industry accounted for 23% of sales and 36% of incremental costs.

By contrast, the communications industry accounted for 13% of sales, 43% of capital expenditures, and 25% of the employees, but incurred less than 1% of the EPA incremental costs for the 48 companies, and the machinery except electrical industry accounted for 7% of sales, 7% of capital expenditures, 10% of employees, but less than 2% of the incremental costs.

The seven areas of high cost regulation shown in Figure 7.13 accounted for 94%, or $1.9 billion, of EPA incremental costs. Over 60% of these are attributable to the Air Program and more than 30% to the Water Program. Two regulations alone—Motor Vehicle Emission (Title 40 CFR, Chapter 1, Parts 85 and 86) and the National Ambient Air Quality Standards That Relate to Particulates (Title 40 CFR, Chapter 1, Part 50)—represent $900 million of incremental costs.

In 1977, to comply with EPA regulations participating com-

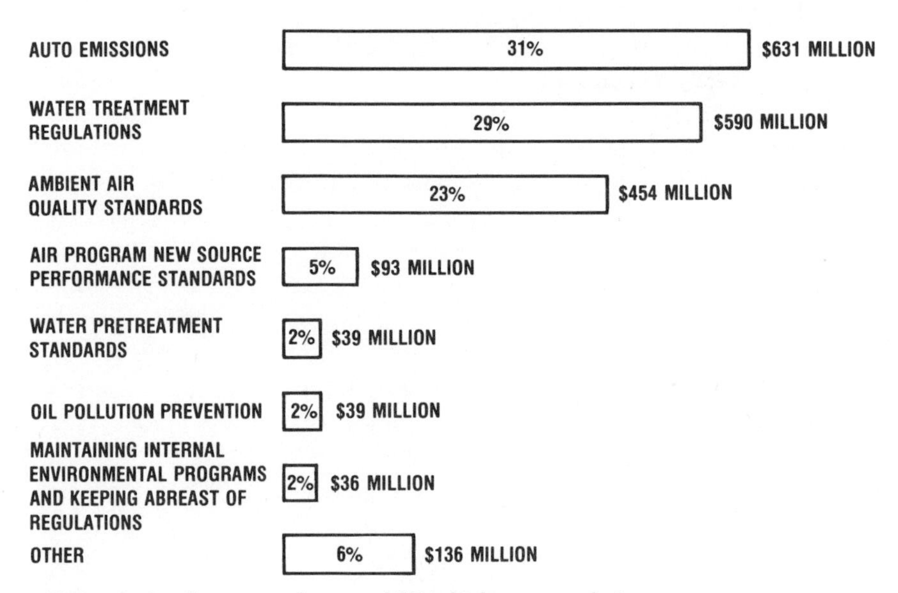

Figure 7.13. Incremental costs of EPA high cost regulations.

panies incurred $623 million of incremental operating and administrative costs. Forty-one participating companies reported labor and nonlabor costs separately. For those companies, the labor element of operating and administrative cost, $203 million, is equivalent to 9000 full-time employees.

The complexity and volume of EPA regulations made it necessary for companies to incur $36 million, primarily in salaried labor costs, solely to maintain internal environmental programs and to keep current with existing regulations and practices and to prepare for new regulations.

The incremental research and development costs incurred by the participating companies to comply with EPA regulations totaled $75 million. Although overall this was only 1% of the total research and development costs for the companies in the study, for those in the chemicals and allied products industry it was equivalent to 5% of their total research and development expenditures in 1977.

Companies reported that although reasonable measures should be taken to protect the environment, small increments of improvement are frequently obtained at great cost. For example, in the mid 1960s a company installed precipitators for the collection of fly ash that removed approximately 95% of the particulates emitted from one of its plants. To comply with the Clean Air Act Amendments, and the requirements of the state implementation plan required by Title 40 CFR, Chapter 1, Part 50, Sections 50.6 and 50.7, the company was required to increase its efficiency so that 99.4% of the particulate matter was removed. Because this degree of efficiency could not be achieved with the existing precipitators it was necessary to replace them with new ones at approximately twice the cost of the original precipitators. The net reduction of less than 5% in particulate emission was achieved at twice the cost needed to achieve the first 95%.

Companies reported that requirements emanating from EPA air regulations (Title 40 CFR, Chapter 1, Part 60, Section 60.45) call for the installation and operation of continuous monitors on new stationary sources of emission and the reporting of resulting data.

As more and more new sources are installed, additional manpower is required to service the monitors and report excess emissions, and additional EPA manpower is required to receive, analyze, and maintain the data. Companies stated that routine compliance observations could serve to disclose significant violations without the installation and operation of expensive continuous monitoring equipment.

One of the electric utilities in the study reported that substantial indirect costs were incurred as a result of delays in obtaining permits for water discharge in a nuclear power plant under construction. During the period of construction, EPA regulations caused significant construction delays through delayed decisions and amended previous decisions. As a result, a large sum of investment capital was unproductive for an extended period of time and the power generation facility was late in becoming operational.

Oil and gas companies identified examples of delays that resulted in costs impacting the entire economy. One such example cited was the Trans-Alaska Pipeline which was delayed over 4 years. The cost of construction was estimated by one of the companies to have increased $3.4 billion due to inflation during this period. Additionally, the companies observed that payments for imported crude oil which North Slope production would have displaced increased the nation's trade deficit by some $20 billion. Another example cited was crude oil production from the Santa Barbara Channel, which has been delayed 5 years with still no assurance as to when production might begin. Oil and gas companies estimate that to date this has cost the nation $500 million in payments for foreign crude.

EQUAL EMPLOYMENT OPPORTUNITY

The incremental cost incurred by participating companies to comply with EEO regulations was $217 million. Of those costs, 96% were operating and administrative, as shown in Figure 7.14.

Two industries—communications and machinery except elec-

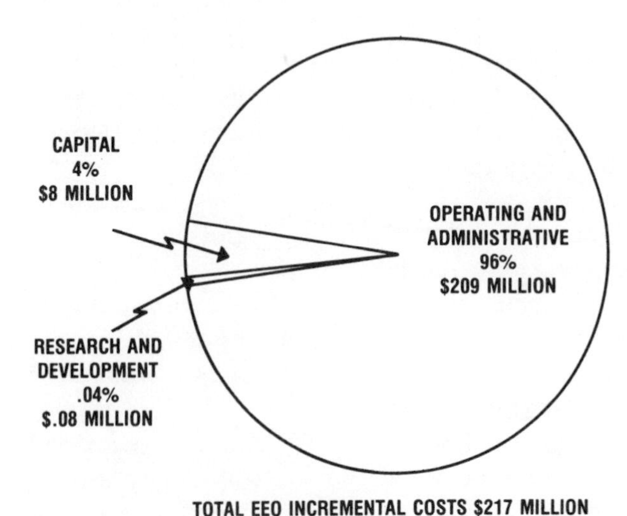

Figure 7.14. EEO incremental costs summarized in three classifications.

trical—accounted for 65% of EEO incremental costs. However, these two industries represent only 40% of the employees of participating companies. EEO incremental costs ranged from approximately $10 per employee per annum in several industries to approximately $150 per employee per annum in the communications industry.

Six areas of regulation account for 95% of the costs to comply with EEO. Figure 7.15 shows an analysis of high cost regulation. Of the costs, $165 million, or 76%, are attributable to affirmative action programs for minorities and women.

Of EEO incremental costs, $165 million, or 76%, are for labor. This is the equivalent of more than 6000 full-time employees of the participating companies.

The EEO regulations required the participating companies to complete more than three million pages of information in 1977 in order to supply and maintain records that provide proof of compliance. Participating companies reported that EEO recordkeeping and reporting requirements are inflexible, and make inadequate allowance for companies with proper records of acceptable affirmative action.

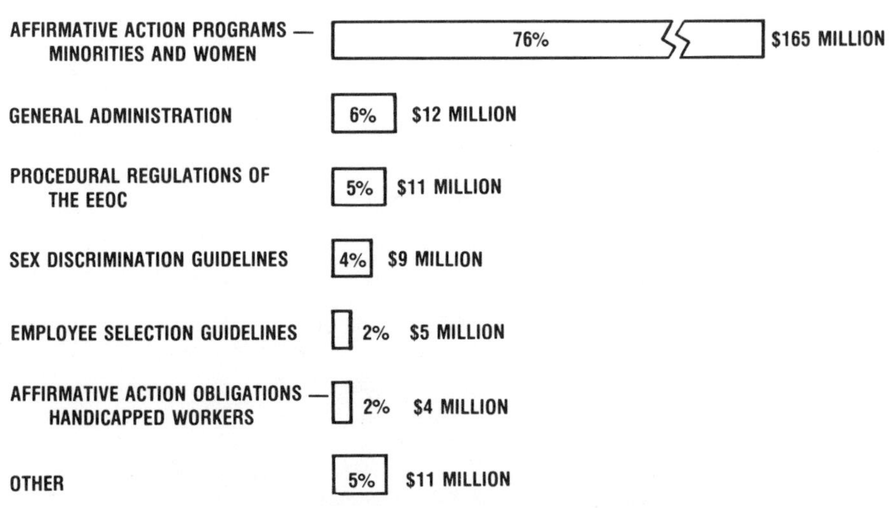

Figure 7.15. Incremental costs of EEO high cost regulations.

The affirmative action program for handicapped workers caused low incremental costs in 1977. Companies reported that of the total $8 million in incremental capital costs, they incurred $1.5 million of incremental capital cost to ensure that new facilities would accommodate the physical limitations of handicapped workers in compliance with CFR Title 41, Chapter 60, Part 60, Subpart A, Section 741.6, Subsection (d). The incremental costs of these regulations in future years are expected to be much larger than those of 1977, particularly with respect to capital expenditures, if companies are required to modify existing facilities.

OCCUPATIONAL SAFETY AND HEALTH ADMINISTRATION

Compliance with the regulations of the Occupational Safety and Health Administration (OSHA) accounted for $184 million of the incremental costs incurred by participating companies. Figure 7.16 shows the distribution of this total by classification of cost.

The relatively low incremental costs attributable to OSHA in 1977 are explained by the fact that many OSHA regulations which

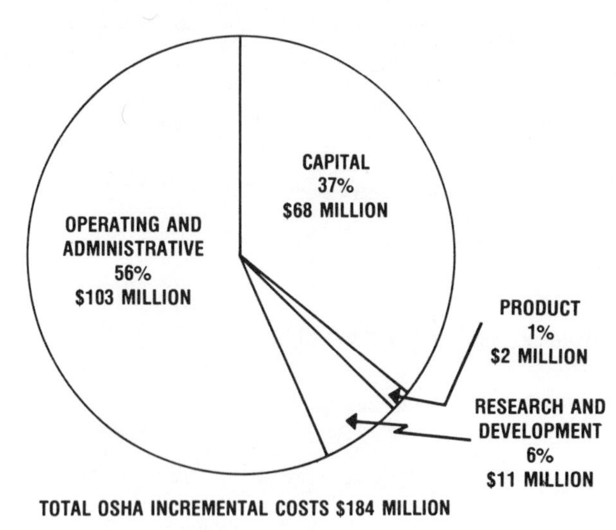

Figure 7.16. OSHA incremental costs summarized in four classifications.

were based on national concensus standards were implemented in the early 1970s. The heaviest expenditures were therefore incurred before 1977. Companies also reported that their total expenditures in 1977 for employee safety and health were many times larger than the cost of those actions they identified as incremental for purposes of this study. For example, the participating companies have provided workers with such items as safety shoes, goggles, and hard hats and have equipped their factories with certain fire suppression equipment and other extensive safety systems for many years. The cost of such actions, although considered in other studies as being incurred to comply with OSHA regulations, were not reported in this study as incremental costs of compliance because such actions would have been taken in the absence of OSHA regulations.

Three industries—chemicals and allied products, rubber and miscellaneous products, and primary metals—accounted for 52% of OSHA incremental costs. However, they represent only 18% of the employees of the participating companies. This illustrates the significant differences in incremental cost impact of OSHA among industries, ranging from $6 per employee per annum in the banking industry and $11 per employee in the communications industry to $220 per employee per annum in the chemical industry.

The six high cost areas of OSHA regulation that account for the majority of the incremental costs are shown in Figure 7.17.

Of incremental OSHA costs, $60 million are attributable to the toxic and hazardous substances regulations, and 68% of these costs were reported by two industries—chemicals and allied products and primary metals. According to companies, incremental costs for these regulations are relatively high compared to other regulations for two major reasons:

1. Many companies consider OSHA's insistence on the use of engineering controls, rather than personal protective equipment, to be inordinately expensive in view of the prescribed exposure levels. In the absence of regulation, companies reported that they could have achieved the same results by the use of face masks and respirators before resorting to equipment modifications and ventilation systems.
2. Companies consider present exposure levels established by

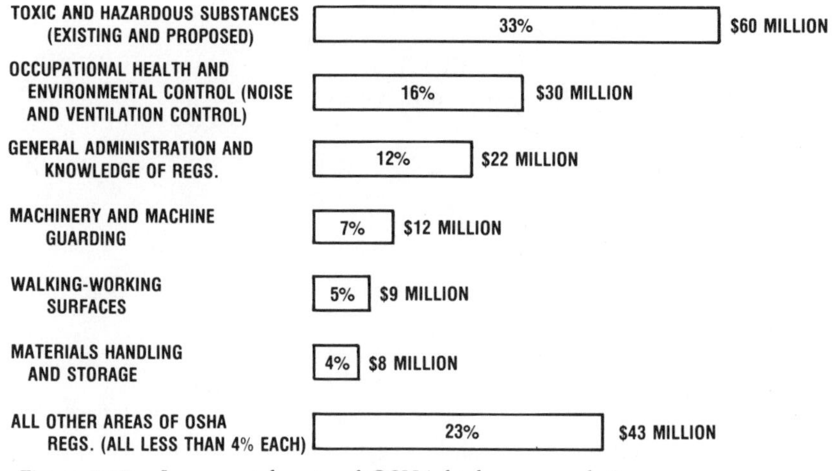

Figure 7.17. Incremental costs of OSHA high cost regulations.

OSHA for toxic substances to be, in many cases, based on insufficient toxicology studies.

The second highest cost area of OSHA regulation was "occupational health and environmental control." OSHA standards dealing with worker exposure to noise are included in this area of regulation and account for the majority of the $30 million reported as incremental cost. Companies reported no strong disagreement with the present tolerable noise level prescribed by OSHA. However, many do not agree with OSHA's insistence upon "feasible engineering controls" to control worker exposure to noise, when the companies have proven personal protective equipment to be both effective and less costly.

Companies reported significant incremental costs for these OSHA regulations because they perceive little relationship between the compliance actions they were forced to take to comply with OSHA's detailed specification standards and the improvement of worker safety. For example, one company reported that over several years it spent more than $400,000 replacing or modifying ladders to meet OSHA specifications; however, to the best of its knowledge, it had not had a reportable incident resulting from the use of such ladders during the past 10 years.

Approximately 900 standards were recently revoked by OSHA. Analysis of the revoked standards indicates that participating companies incurred small amounts of incremental costs in 1977 in complying with the standards. However, the action by OSHA is perceived by the companies as an important first step in the simplification of regulations and elimination of unnecessary requirements wherever possible.

DEPARTMENT OF ENERGY

Incremental costs incurred by participating companies to comply with Department of Energy (DOE) regulations in 1977 were $116 million, 60% of which were operating and administrative. Figure 7.18 shows an analysis of the classification of costs. Participating companies collected costs of complying with regulations of the Federal Energy Administration and Federal Power Commission, two agencies that were merged into the Department of Energy.

The incremental costs of complying with DOE regulations are considered by many companies, particularly those in the oil and gas industry, to be very small in relation to the costs of the secondary effects of these regulations. They assert that market distortions and inefficiencies are associated with crude oil and petroleum product allocations and price controls and that they far outweigh the incremental costs of complying with these regulations. The oil and gas companies also observed that price controls have resulted in disincentives to increased domestic production of crude oil and natural gas, investment in sour crude refining capacity, and investment in facilities to upgrade octane-producing capability, but have encouraged increased consumption. The net effect is to increase the nation's reliance on unstable foreign

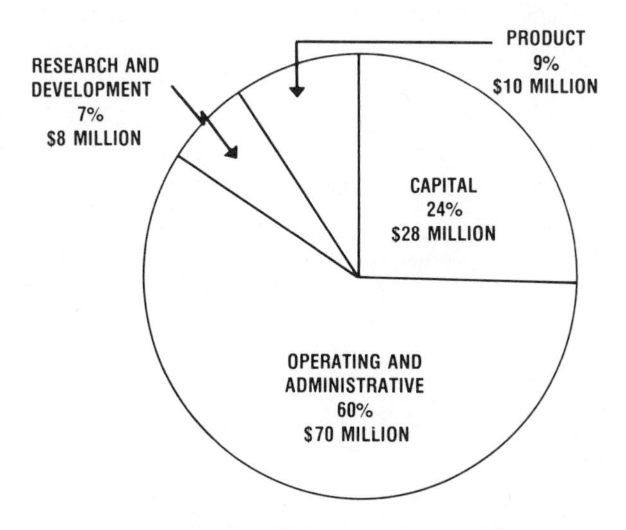

Figure 7.18. DOE incremental costs summarized in four classifications.

sources of supply, while contributing to the balance of payments deficit and the decline of the dollar in international markets. They point out that none of these very real costs of regulation are reflected in the incremental costs reported in this study for DOE.

Incremental capital costs of $28 million were incurred in 1977 to comply with DOE regulations. Completion of capital projects that were started in 1977 will consume another $126 million of incremental costs in years after 1977. More than $40 million of incremental recurring operating costs will be required annually in the oil and gas industry alone to operate capital projects active in 1977 when they become operational.

Four industries—oil and gas, electrical machinery, transportation equipment, and electric and gas services—incurred the highest relative incremental costs to comply with DOE regulations in 1977.

The oil and gas industry accounted for 21% of sales but 33% of incremental costs, the electrical machinery industry accounted for 8% of sales and 28% of incremental costs, the transportation equipment industry accounted for 20% of sales and 17% of incremental costs, and the electric and gas services industry accounted for 1% of sales and 2% of incremental costs. Together, they accounted for 80% of the incremental costs incurred by the participating companies, but only 50% of their sales, 35% of capital expenditures, and 36% of employees.

The five high costs areas of DOE regulation are shown in Figure 7.19. They relate to DOE's fuel usage and pricing, energy conservation programs, and administration.

In the fuel category, natural gas usage regulations accounted for incremental costs of $35 million. Of the costs, 54% were incremental capital costs associated with the installation of alternate fuel facilities as a result of required curtailments of natural gas or the installation of multiple fuel capabilities in anticipation of such curtailments.

Price controls on natural gas were cited by the oil and gas industry as one of the reasons that curtailments were necessary. The low price of natural gas relative to other fuels has encouraged its

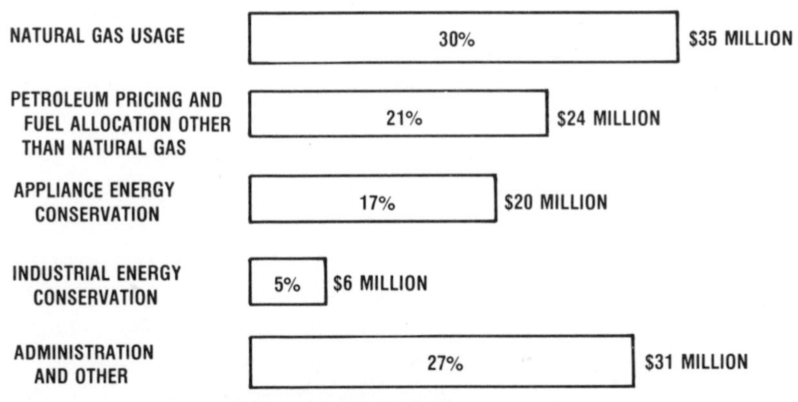

Figure 7.19. Incremental costs of DOE high cost regulations.

use and discouraged conservation. In addition, they reported that controls have limited the incentives to find and produce more natural gas, contributing further to the supply and demand imbalance. Thus, they considered the most significant cost of natural gas regulations to be the cost that was not calculated in the study—the long-term impacts on the U.S. economy.

Many companies reported their concern over the inherent conflict in the objectives of the DOE and the EPA in the natural gas area. In 1977, DOE was striving toward the use of coal rather than natural gas, while the EPA was attempting to control coal stack emissions. Coal is not as clean burning as natural gas, and its use intensified the concerns over ambient air quality.

Twenty million dollars of incremental costs, of which approximately 50% were product costs, were incurred to make home appliances, predominantly refrigerators and freezers, more energy efficient.

All of these costs were incurred by companies in the electrical machinery manufacturing industry. Estimated capital expenditures of $24 million after 1977 to complete projects costing $4 million in 1977 indicate a possible sharp increase in incremental costs for this program in future years.

Companies, mainly in the petroleum industry, reported $24

million of incremental costs relating to pricing administration, crude and product allocations, and the filing of reports with the DOE. No estimate has been made of the even greater secondary effects associated with these regulations.

Many of the actions taken by companies to comply with the DOE's energy conservation regulations were initiated for sound business reasons and were not considered to be incremental costs of regulation. The incremental costs—$6 million—associated with the DOE's Industrial Energy Conservation Program represented costs incurred in measuring and reporting energy usage to DOE.

The total incremental costs reported in general administration and other areas were $31 million, more than 90% of which were operating and administrative. These costs represent administrative actions required to stay current with DOE regulations, to maintain accounts as required by the DOE, and to report various types of information to the DOE.

EMPLOYEE RETIREMENT INCOME SECURITY ACT

All of the $61 million incremental Employee Retirement Income Security Act (ERISA) costs in 1977 were classified as operating and administrative. They resulted from increased reporting to government or plan participants or from increased payments to pension plans and the Pension Benefit Guaranty Corporation.

Figure 7.20 shows the incremental costs for the five high cost ERISA regulations.

As a result of ERISA's higher standards for vesting, participation, and benefit accruals, participating companies incurred incremental costs of $40 million. The costs, which represent additional contributions by the companies to their employee pension plans for future distribution to retirees, constitute only one-half of 1% of total 1977 pension and profit-sharing contributions by the companies. The most costly compliance actions related to the acceleration of vesting of participants' accrued benefits and the revisions of eligibility requirements for participation.

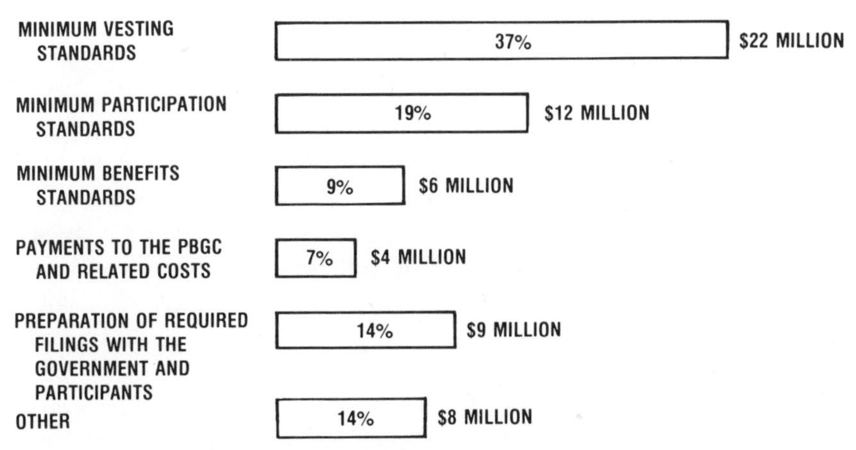

Figure 7.20. Incremental costs of ERISA high cost regulations.

The incremental administrative costs of ERISA are disproportionately greater for smaller businesses than for larger businesses. For example, the 10 smallest employers incurred average incremental costs per employee in 1977 nearly seven times those of the 10 largest. This may be a factor that has discouraged the development of private pension systems, as is evident by the fall in ratio of new plans to terminated plans from 14.4 to 1 in 1973 to 2.2 to 1 in 1977.

FEDERAL TRADE COMMISSION

Consumer protection regulations in 1977 imposed incremental costs of $26 million on participating companies. The $26 million includes $3 million of costs collected by the bank participants which are under the jurisdiction of the Federal Reserve System.

Although the study methodology enabled firms to report incremental costs in any aspect of Federal Trade Commission (FTC) activity, only those pertaining to the Bureau of Consumer Protection were reported by enough companies to allow for significant analysis and discussion.

A number of companies with significant costs related to the Bureau of Competition did not choose to report these costs. The Department of Justice has overlapping jurisdiction with the FTC in antitrust enforcement, and consequently many companies believed that it would be impossible to draw meaningful conclusions in the antitrust area. As a result, the data collected on this aspect of FTC activity were incomplete and represented only a portion of the costs related to FTC antitrust matters. For those companies that did report incremental costs in this area, the total amounted to approximately $23 million.

All consumer credit related costs and most other costs were operating and administrative. These costs were incurred to modify systems and procedures, train employees, and provide required customer disclosures under the truth in lending and equal credit opportunity regulations. Capital and research and development costs relate to research to support product disclosure claims either required by a consent decree or contemplated by proposed regulations. Figure 7.21 shows the FTC cost classification.

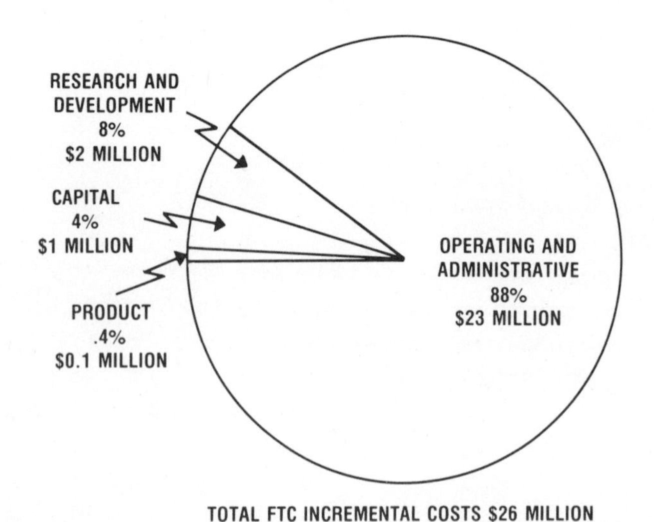

Figure 7.21. FTC incremental costs summarized in four classifications.

Three industries—banks, credit agencies other than banks, and stone, clay, glass, and concrete products—incurred the highest relative incremental costs to comply with consumer protection regulations in 1977. Banks with 4% of the sales of the participating companies accounted for 11% of incremental costs to comply with these regulations. Credit agencies other than banks accounted for 1% of sales and 42% of incremental costs. Stone, clay, glass, and concrete products accounted for 1% of sales and 7% of incremental costs.

Consumer credit regulations which include truth in lending, equal credit opportunity, and fair credit reporting accounted for $15 million of the $23 million FTC consumer protection costs reported. Figure 7.22 shows incremental costs for each high cost regulation.

Costs of truth in lending disclosures in particular were considered to be excessive in light of their perceived benefit. The detailed semiannual customer statement of rights in case of billing disputes was cited as unnecessary, particularly considering the number of credit cards and other consumer credit accounts of the average consumer. Truth in lending cost of credit disclosures were considered by many participants to have evolved to such a state

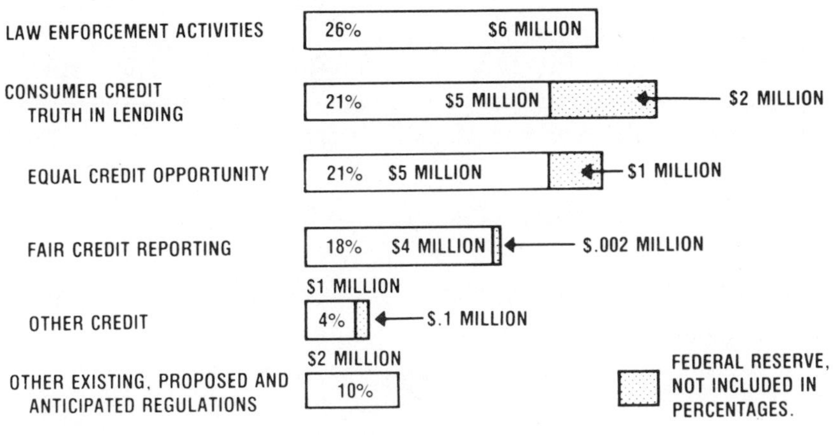

Figure 7.22. Incremental costs of FTC high cost regulations.

of complexity that the disclosures may actually detract from consumer understanding.

As expected from the outset, incremental costs of FTC compliance were low in comparison to other agencies studied. Concerns expressed by the participants dealt more with potential danger from the misuse of enforcement authority and from potential disclosure of proprietary information than with the direct cost of compliance.

USE OF THE STUDY RESULTS

The Business Roundtable, the participating member companies, and Arthur Andersen & Co. have made a significant investment to produce specific and documented regulatory cost data and a methodology that can be useful in improving the regulatory policymaking process.

Although considerable analysis of the data has already been performed in the writing of this report, further analysis by business, government, academic institutions, and other interested groups is encouraged.

The results produced by the study and the proven methodology for cost determination can now be used to benefit business, government, and the consumer.

By focusing their attention on the existing high cost regulations and on proposed regulations having high cost attributes, those interested in reform can use the study data presented in several ways:

- To determine better methods of achieving regulatory objectives at lower cost to the economy
- To evaluate and, where appropriate, modify regulatory procedures and standards
- To stimulate additional studies of other business sectors, specific industries, specific regulations and benefits

The Business Roundtable and Arthur Andersen & Co. are

prepared to assist and work with the regulatory agencies, the executive and legislative branches of government, industry and trade associations, and other interested groups in conducting further analysis of the results and performing similar studies using the proven study methodology.

Without a doubt, the recent trend in government regulation has been toward greater involvement of government in business activity. Government has imposed high cost regulations to achieve social goals and, as indicated in this study, the costs will grow. The best hope for reform lies in the changes in attitude that seem to be taking place toward regulation, both in the private and public sectors. Political leaders, business groups, and private citizens in growing numbers are expressing the need for an improved regulatory system. No one can dispute the fact that regulations have resulted in some valuable and beneficial gains for society. Still, most agree there is much room for improvement. The objective of this study is to contribute to the body of knowledge necessary for making rational judgments in determining the best balance between regulatory goals and the costs the nation must bear in pursuing them.

PART III

THE PROBLEM OF REFORM

CHAPTER **8**

The Distressing Relationship between Government and Business

THOMAS A. MURPHY

I do not get a chance to spend as much time as I would like in an academic atmosphere or in New England, but this seems to be my week to make up for that. I had a brief meeting at Smith College this morning, then here in Burlington this afternoon, and I am scheduled to be back in Boston this weekend. I feel a bit like a candidate in the primaries who somehow lost a week on his calendar.

I hasten to add I am not a candidate for any office, including the one I now hold and for which I will no longer be eligible after this year. I stress that because I think in the last few weeks you have all probably heard enough political speeches to last you for a while. So, this will *not* be a political talk. But it will be about politics . . . at least according to Webster's definition, which says politics is "the art or science of government (or) of guiding or influencing governmental policy."

Specifically, I would like to offer a few thoughts on the subject of government and business, and, more specifically, on the

ISBN 0-12-277620-8 0-12-277622-4(p)

regulatory climate within which every business in the nation must operate.

It seems to be more or less widely held, at least among some in the business community today, that government regulation of business is something relatively new and something totally unjustified. Neither of these notions is true.

From the earliest days of our nation, business has had to operate within the framework of law, and nobody would have it otherwise. We formally recognized the need for this relationship nearly 200 years ago, when we ratified a Constitution which gave Congress the power to "regulate commerce with foreign nations and among the several states. . . ."

The only relatively new aspect in this relationship is the growth, in the last 15 years or so, of what almost amounts to a fourth branch of government. When I was in school, the textbooks discussed the executive branch, the judicial branch, and the legislative branch. Perhaps they still do. But today we have a fourth branch—the regulatory agencies—which, to some extent, whether by accident or by design, are outside the purview of the other three.

The concept of regulatory agencies began to grow in the 1930s, a period that marked a dramatic shift in America from a reliance on an adaptation of English common law to a growing reliance on the authority of Congress. One of the ways in which Congress chose to deal with this new authority was by establishing a number of regulatory agencies. Remember, it was a time of worldwide depression, and the government was attempting to respond to the economic and social upheaval of the times. There was a perceived need to eliminate or moderate economic downturns, and the result was a surge of economic regulation.

Today, after a decade of the most explosive growth of regulation in history, not even the government itself is certain how many agencies it has created. In 1979, President Carter reported to Congress that there were 90 such agencies. A year earlier, the General Accounting Office concluded there were 116.

The charters of these agencies frequently put them beyond the reach of either the Administration or the Congress and some have judiciary powers, giving them in effect a charter not only to set the rules, but to act as prosecutor, as judge, and as jury in the enforcement of those rules.

We have seen almost the same regulatory explosion at the state and local levels of government. This proliferation is, in my opinion, a symptom of a rather serious national malady: the idea that every problem can and must be solved by the government—by enacting a new law, by establishing a new agency for its administration, and by hiring another 5000 people to grind out another 50,000 pages of regulation. We are certainly a nation of law, but I have some trouble with the concept of a separate law for every past, present, and future aspect of our personal and professional lives. Someone has said that more than 30,000 laws and countless regulations have been enacted in a vain attempt to implement the Ten Commandments.

However, we must remember that laws and regulations are not inherently objectionable. Government regulation of business, or of any other activity, becomes objectionable only when that regulation is excessive and unwarranted. Nobody, in my experience, has ever advocated an end to all government involvement in our lives. No sensible person would say that there should be no traffic safety laws. No sensible person would argue that some products, such as uranium, should not be regulated.

Our society and every other society in the world has some situations which bear upon the health and welfare of both the individual and the general populace where regulation of some sort is not only desirable but absolutely necessary.

But all of us are entitled to a reasoned approach to government regulation. We are entitled to an approach to regulation that is not wasteful of human resources and of our tax dollars. We are entitled to balanced regulation, regulation that does not hinder the growth of our national economy. Most importantly, we all are entitled to our individual freedom subject to the reasonable rules of a prudent society—individual freedom that should not be sacrificed in the name of needless government control.

But, too often, all of those things to which you and I are entitled are lost when government imposes another law or another regulation. We lose those entitlements when laws and regulations are not based on factual research. We lose when the government regulates without input from those to be regulated. We lose when the decisions of the government are based on only emotional considerations or on political expediency. We lose when government decisions fail to take into account the cost of regulation compared to the expected benefits. Perhaps above all, we lose when there is no real need for the law or regulation in the first place.

Let me give you one concrete example of how we lose at the hands of excessive government regulation. From 1974 through 1978, to comply or to prepare to comply with regulations imposed by all levels of government, General Motors spent almost $1.2 billion a year. Our figures for 1979 are not complete, but we anticipate the result will be similar—another $1 billion or more, for a 6-year total of nearly $7.5 billion. These expenditures represent a cost of roughly $200 for each and every car we produce each year. Yet they do not include the cost of equipment added to our products to meet government-mandated requirements—equipment that has increased by more than $600 the cost of a typical car in recent years. Nor do these expenditures include anything we have spent to improve the fuel economy of our cars. We have achieved a fuel economy improvement of almost 80% since 1974 in response to consumer demands—not because of government requirements.

Now, admittedly, General Motors is a fairly sizable organization. Not every business today is spending a billion dollars a year complying with regulation. But every business is spending something. And to the extent that at least a portion of that something is unnecessary, you and I and every other American consumer are paying more than we should for the products we use. Ironically, we also bear additional taxes to pay for the regulators who imposed those costs on us.

Of course, while you and I are paying more for a product which may carry little or no increase in real value, there are those in government who are trying their best to figure out how to curb inflation. I would like to add my support to a recommendation the Carter administration made with respect to government regulation, specifically as regulation contributes to today's inflationary pressures. The recommendation is this: that government take a very close look at its degree of involvement in business and critically evaluate which areas of involvement are really required and beneficial to the American public and which areas foster benefits that outweigh the cost of government involvement.

Those laws and regulations that pass such an evaluation should be retained. But there are also areas in which government involvement is neither necessary nor beneficial, which merely add unnecessarily to the burden of business and to costs for the consumer. Those areas of government involvement should be reduced at least and eliminated at best—not just for the benefit of business, but for the nation's benefit, for the people's benefit. Simply, government should not needlessly regulate those it purports to govern.

Some regulation goes beyond the needless and can have adverse affects on health. Recently, for example, the Department of Energy reportedly refused to allow the University of Washington to raise the thermostats in the school's art building—despite the fact that the nude models were freezing to death.

An even better example of the morass of regulation that applies to colleges and universities lies in the story told by Mr. L. William Seidman, who served as President Ford's economic advisor. It seems that the president of Mr. Seidman's alma mater called him in desperation one day. As the beleagured president spoke, two government officials were in his office, one from the Internal Revenue Service and one from Health, Education and Welfare, and, together, they presented quite a problem. The IRS man said that the college was required to keep all applications received on file in order to prove that there had been no discrimination in the admissions procedure. The HEW man, on the other hand, said that the college must destroy all applications of people who had not been accepted in order to prevent lifelong unfavorable marks from being placed on their records. The college president wanted Seidman's advice. The best Seidman could do was to say, "Well, you have both of the gentlemen there—speak to them about this and see if they can't reconcile it." To this the president replied, "Well I have talked with them, and they said this: 'You can have your choice. You can lose your tax exemption if you want to follow the HEW plan or, if you would rather lose all the federal grants you are receiving, you can follow the IRS plans.'"

I am a bit more familiar with automobiles than academics, so I would like to use an example from my industry to illustrate the kind of regulation that is necessary and the kind of regulation that is questionable. The example involves automobile emissions.

There is simply no question that clean air is necessary. Nor was there any question, some years ago, that automotive emissions detracted from that desirable goal. Something had to be done to reduce emissions levels, and—in this case—market forces alone would not accomplish that. In other words, pollution control systems were not salable. I think the logic of the typical car owner was something like this: If the owners of every other car in my neighborhood paid for emission control devices, it would cause little harm if I refused to do so. Conversely, if nobody else agreed to pay the extra price, why should I?

We saw an excellent example of this thinking in Arizona a few years ago. We offered the public a retro-fit emission control system which could easily be installed in older automobiles and which would dramatically reduce tailpipe emissions. The price was less than $100, and we advertised the system in a weeks-long campaign. I think we sold six of them.

So, in the case of automotive emissions, it obviously was necessary to enact some laws, some regulations, to achieve a goal that would protect the health of all Americans. Nobody argued with the need for the regulation. But there was a great deal of concern about how the government arrived at what it considered reasonable emissions levels.

Rather than base the acceptable levels on scientific evaluations of potential health effects, Congress—in the Clean Air Act of

1970—decreed that emissions of carbon monoxide, of hydrocarbons, and of oxides of nitrogen be reduced by 90% from levels then existing. Was it necessary to push for standards that come so close to the zero level? Did the effects on health require this sort of reduction? Since sufficient scientific studies were never made, those questions remained unanswered. Nevertheless, the standards were set. Ten years later we have spent, and are spending, billions of dollars to reach those objectives without any determination of whether they are necessary for health and despite their negative effects on fuel conservation.

There is another aspect of regulation that deserves especially serious study given the continuing international trade deficit. There seems to be a tendency, in some proposed regulation, to favor foreign interests over American interests. Consider, for example, a proposal concerning fuel economy standards. Although the major domestic companies are required to meet the fuel economy standards every year, some small-volume companies which produce fewer than 10,000 vehicles a year have received much more lenient standards. The Department of Transportation has proposed that, in the future, such manufacturers be *totally exempt* from compliance with the standards. It has also been proposed that the law be changed to permit foreign companies that began manufacturing operations in the United States after 1975 to import freely any vehicles they manufacture outside the United States and include them for purposes of determining their fleet fuel economy average. On the other hand, the established domestic manufacturers cannot import vehicles and count them for this purpose unless the vehicles have at least 75% American content. Obviously, this gives a break to Volkswagen—and it would offer the same advantage to Japanese companies that reportedly are considering setting up plants in this country.

There is also an element of discrimination in the proposed standards for diesel particulates in automotive emissions. As they now stand, these standards would be much more difficult to meet in the larger engines found in American-built cars than in the smaller ones built by overseas competitors.

As a final example, I would like to mention the passive-restraint requirements. Smaller, two- and four-passenger cars (in other words, the vast majority of imports) are not required to have such systems until 1984. However, by 1982, 2 years earlier, full-size cars, which are almost the exclusive domain of American manufacturers, will be required to have such extra-cost systems. This extra cost will result in higher prices for these American-built cars, as will the staggering costs incurred in researching, testing, and developing the highly sophisticated inflatable restraint systems that will be installed as optional equipment in many of them, specifically those designed to accommodate six passengers.

The point of all this is that the discretionary powers, as well as the statutory powers, assigned to the regulatory agencies of our government are frequently putting American business and industry at a distinct and unfortunate disadvantage in world trade. This occurs not just in overseas areas, but right here in our home market—the only truly international market anywhere in the world today. It is the largest market, the most attractive, and the most freely accessible to all producers.

In my opinion, much of the problem derives from the fact that Congress has created too many regulatory agencies which were assigned one mission and one mission only. As a result, each agency tends to look upon the work of other agencies as completely extraneous to its own work. Points of conflict develop and are ignored; and no one seems to care about the cumulative cost effects that are produced upon business, the consumers, or the nation.

There is much talk in Washington about regulatory reform but, frankly, we at General Motors see little in the way of concrete results. Reform or no reform, our regulatory costs continue to mount and so does the number of people we must assign for no other productive purpose than to achieve company compliance. Still, we have hopes. There are three results that we especially hope will come out of any reform movement.

First, our regulatory agencies must be compelled to discard their "one-mission" approach and take into consideration the spillover effects of all standard setting on the attainment of other social and economic objectives in this nation. Second, more use must be made of third-party studies and reports to eliminate conflicts between one regulation and another and to keep their costs more in line with their benefits. Third, the depth, scope, and intensity of the judiciary's review of regulations must be increased without relying so heavily on the "expertise" of the regulatory agencies.

Of course, the progress of the regulatory reform movement will depend almost completely on the relationship that exists between government and business. Over the past half-century or so, that relationship has not been exactly smooth and unruffled. Business has been accused of exerting too much power over government officials; there has been distrust of major corporations, particularly those with extensive international operations; the word "profit" has been twisted into a synonym for greed and antisocial materialism.

The business community, meanwhile, has only recently made an attempt to counter such charges and movements in a constructive way. Heretofore, it was too often satisfied to remain silent and to refuse to enter the ideological arena. When it did speak up, it was too often in a shrill, "government-be-damned" voice. In addition, some businesses compounded the problem by ignoring responsibilities and creating large numbers of dissatisfied and militant consumers.

However, as I indicated, business is now taking a more enlightened and constructive approach to this problem. For several years, at every opportunity I get, I have been preaching the gospel of business–government cooperation and of an end to the old adversary climate. And I have not been alone. Virtually every major executive at every major corporation I know of believes as I do. And, I think we are winning the battle in the business community. We are gaining support for a more reasoned and less rhetorical attitude toward government.

Some in government feel the same way, and we hope that the elections of 1980 will see their numbers increase. This country urgently needs more statesmen in government and fewer adversaries, fewer anti-business zealots. I am thinking particularly of those who seem bent upon always casting business in the role of villain, as the source of all our country's troubles. In the long run, such single-minded people may lose their credibility and their influence. Meanwhile, they are capable of great damage. This country can ill afford the bitter price of the adversary climate these zealots have committed themselves to preserve and to advance. We in American industry cannot afford to tackle the world marketplace without our government on our side. We simply cannot compete effectively against foreign manufacturers who are being cheered onward by their governments who view them as prime national assets, if at the same time our own government treats its domestic industry as an enemy, to be hampered, held back, whittled down.

We need cooperation, not confrontation, between government and business. We need a sense of unity. We need a common commitment to take the shackles off business and to release all of the competitive power that still exists in American initiative and enterprise.

CHAPTER 9

The Problem of Balancing the Costs and Benefits of Regulation: Two Views

ALLEN R. FERGUSON
MURRAY L. WEIDENBAUM

MURRAY L. WEIDENBAUM

The nature of business–government relations has undergone many dramatic changes in the last 20 years. Perhaps the most significant has been the shift from the notion of a specific industry regulated by a single commission (i.e., utilities by public service boards, railroads and trucking by the Interstate Commerce Commission [ICC], etc.) to a situation in which regulatory agencies such as the Occupational Safety and Health Administration (OSHA) and the Environmental Protection Agency (EPA) regulate specific activities of all firms, regardless of the industry in which the individual firms operate. If you were to rank industries by the intensity of regulations, those which have been in the past the most heavily regulated (utilities, railroads, and the airlines before deregulation) would not be very high on the list today. On top of the list I think you would find the petroleum, the chemical, the aerospace, and health services industries. These are all high technology areas. Most of these firms are manufacturers, and they

ISBN 0-12-277620-8 0-12-277622-4(p)

are all subject to an array of government regulations. You still have the Interstate Commerce Commission, of course, regulating the railroads and truckers. But you do not have a chemical industry regulatory commission. You do not have an aerospace regulatory commission. Instead, you have a host of regulations from a variety of agencies determining the way in which these firms operate. Unfortunately, the new forms of regulation are not a substitute for the old forms; instead, they are superimposed upon the old, a situation that makes the analysis of the impact of regulation far more difficult.

In the past, economists and political scientists developed what was called the "capture theory" to explain the process and result of regulation. In essence, the theory held that while the ICC regulated the railroads and truckers, the ICC's constituency was the very group of firms it regulated. Similarly, for years prior to airline deregulation, I used to say that the Civil Aeronautics Board (CAB) did not worry so much about me as a passenger as it did about the health and well being of the airline industry. The same comment would apply to the ICC, the old Federal Power Commission (which is now the Federal Energy Regulatory Commission), and so on. This has led to the amusing situation of the regulated firm being one of the most vocal opponents of eliminating the old-style regulation. For instance, the airlines and their unions opposed the phasing-out of the CAB route and fare regulations. The railroads and trucking firms and their respective unions have taken the same stance with respect to reducing the scope of ICC authority over their industries.

The situation is far different with the younger generation of regulatory agencies. The EPA is concerned with the impact on the environment of the activity of virtually any unit—from General Motors down to pleasure boaters on coastal and inland waters. The Consumer Product Safety Commission (CPSC) is charged with overseeing the safety of virtually all consumer products from all industries. OSHA is concerned with workplace safety and health across the board. The Equal Employment Opportunity

Commission (EEOC) covers discrimination and personnel practices of all firms, public and private.

For these reasons, then, the concept of the regulated firm "capturing" the regulatory body is simply not applicable here. However, there is a parallel in that these newer agencies also have their own constituencies, though they are far different from those of the old. It is not the regulated industry, but the "public interest" movement which spawned the agencies. The EPA responds to the environmental movement, Friends of the Earth, the Sierra Club, and so forth. The CPSC looks to the consumer movement, OSHA to the labor unions, and EEOC to the civil rights groups.

If the old-type agency is too concerned with the well-being of the industry it regulates, no one can argue that EPA or OSHA are too concerned with the financial health of the firms they control. At times, the EPA has measured its "accomplishments" in terms of the number of polluting factories closed down. The opportunity simply does not exist for any industry to "capture" one of these new agencies, for the agency regulates far too many different industries. These organizations do not have a great deal of concern with the economic impact of their activity. They look upon the resources of these industries as the wherewithal to achieve their social objectives.

I am not condemning any of these agencies as evil or inherently contrary to the public interest, but I will not put the white hat on any of them, as the media too often does. If we look at government regulation from the point of view of the private sector rather than from that of the government, we find that every industry in this country has become a regulated industry. We also find that the costs of this activity are enormous. I have tried to assess these costs in steps, by dividing the costs according to whether they are direct, indirect, or induced effects of regulation.

The direct effects are the most noticeable and easily measured. They consist in part of the operating expenses of the regulatory agencies, the resources required to promulgate and enforce the regulations of the agencies. This is what we call hard data. You simply sit down with the Budget of the United States Government and its appendix, and you establish the expenditures for each federal program. For the 1980 Budget, this figure comes to $6 billion. A second cost that should also be categorized as direct is the cost to the private sector of actions required by the regulations. Take the case of the passenger automobile. Here the direct costs of regulation would be the price of the seat belt, shoulder harness, shock-absorbing bumpers and steering wheel, the catalytic converter, and all those items required by regulation. These data are also readily available, because each year the Bureau of Labor Statistics, as part of its work on price indices, determines for the average automobile the cost of meeting each new mandate. For 1978, I came up with a cost of about $666 for the average passenger car to meet the health, environmental, and safety regulations.

The second order, or indirect, effects of regulation consist in large measure of the costs of complying with governmental reporting requirements—in a word, paperwork. In the case of a firm's finance department, its work has shifted from simply providing information to management to providing data required by government. If you were to work in the personnel department, you would find a large portion of your time spent keeping your firm out of trouble with the regulators. Keeping abreast of the regulations and filling out affirmative action reports becomes an important function of corporate personnel departments.

The third order, or induced, costs are perhaps the largest and most elusive. I have tried to quantify costs only for the first two categories, and those numbers are very large. Yet it is this third category, whose costs I have not quantified, that frankly worries me the most, for this segment includes the impact of regulation on the dynamism of the economy. Consider the research and development function of a firm. It determines the rate of innovation (the application of scientific developments), which in turn determines productivity growth and new product development. I find a rising share of company research and development being devoted to what is called in the trade "defensive research." That term does not refer to defending the company against its competitors, but against the government. So, when I see a rising share of our scientists and engineers devoting their time to responding to regulation, I am not surprised when I see a diminution of the fruits of research and development. When I look at capital formation (investment in new plant and equipment), I see about 10% of new capital formation going to the antipollution scrubbers on the electric utilities and to similar investments, which are not designed to increase the production of goods and services to be sold to the consumer but, rather, are intended to meet the social requirements imposed by the regulatory agencies.

The opportunity cost of this diversion is very, very high. Edward Dennison of the Department of Commerce has estimated that we lose about one-fourth of the annual potential increase in productivity because of this diversion of capital to those social goals. This slowdown in productivity growth poses serious problems for the future, especially if still other social goals are to be achieved.

Perhaps the most compelling component of the induced effect is what I call the bureaucratization of decisions that results. For instance, under the Employee Retirement Income Security Act (ERISA), pension fund managers are behaving more and more like bureaucrats. They avoid taking risks, avoid investing in new firms; they follow the pack and stick to large, well-known, blue-chip companies. They keep copious records on their pension activities and hire numerous consultants so that they can cover themselves if criticized and thus dilute responsibility.

I have not attempted to put a dollar sign on these induced effects. However, I doubt that they are trivial, given the concurrent slowdown in capital formation, innovation, and productivity growth. I did not forecast the Chrysler problem per se, but I have argued that the smaller companies in every industry will be the hardest hit. There are economies of scale in complying with government regulation, and the sort of questions raised by the Chrysler bailout will surface more frequently. That is not my own personal conjecture. I hosted a group of people from the Library of Congress who sought help in developing general guidelines and national policies for corporate bailouts. They came to me because two different congressional committees had made the same inquiries independently, and the Congress did not wish to continue to receive the hit-or-miss responses that had characterized the cases of Chrysler and Lockheed.

My colleagues and I at the Center for the Study of American Business at Washington University have made an attempt to estimate the magnitude of the first and second order effects of all federal government regulation. In some cases, such as that of automobiles cited earlier and environmental regulation, we used government data as the basis of our estimates. In the case of specific industry regulation, such as utilities, airlines, etc., we surveyed the professional literature using what we thought to be the best available studies. Whenever there was a range, we took the low end, as, given our philosophical biases, we did not want to be accused of "cooking" the results. Of course, the simple fact that we took much of the data from government sources should give our estimates somewhat of a downward bias. Being realistic, we assumed that the data are apt to be biased according to the source. The business community is likely to exaggerate the cost of compliance while understating the benefits. The agencies will tend to do the opposite. This is, unfortunately, normal.

For a number of programs we could not get a handle on the second order costs. Thus, for not so trivial agencies like the Department of Energy, the Nuclear Regulatory Commission, and the Consumer Product Safety Commission, we carried that cost at zero. It is strange, but our critics who argued that our estimates were far too high have always ignored the fact that, in so many cases, rather than guess, we carried the cost of regulation at zero. If anything, most of our errors are underestimations rather than overestimations of cost.

For 1979, these estimates totaled over 100 billion dollars—$102.7 billion, to be exact.

My ultimate purpose in making this estimate has not been so much to quantify the cost as it has been to try to move public policy in the direction of balancing, comparing, and evaluating the benefits and costs that arise from government regulation. There is a normal tendency of proponents of regulation to focus on the benefits and opponents to focus on the cost. I have tried very hard to push public policy away from the two polar extremes to that high middle ground where you compare the costs and benefits of such incremental regulatory activity. The result, as you might suspect, is that I am then attacked from the left because the white-hatted crusaders are skeptical of the green-eyeshade approach to decisions. And, of course, I am attacked from the right because, clearly, if the marginal benefits do exceed the marginal costs, I have provided a rationale for government intervention.

For those libertarians who may read this, let me close by quoting your friend and mine, that wild-eyed leftist, Friedrich von Hayek, from his book, *Constitution of Liberty:*

> A free market system does not exclude on principle . . . all regulations governing the techniques of production. . . . [Regulations] will normally raise the costs of production or, what amounts to the same thing, reduce overall productivity. But if this effect on cost is fully taken into account and it is still thought worthwhile to incur these costs to achieve a given end, there is little more to be said about it. The appropriateness of such measures must be judged by comparing the overall cost with the gain. It cannot be conclusively determined by appeal to a general principle.[1]

I rest my case.

ALLEN R. FERGUSON

I do not want to be cast strictly in the role of rebuttal, because I agree with much of what Murray has said, especially his concluding comments. Certainly neither of us would argue that there should be no regulation. I would agree that there is frequently too much regulation. So the question comes down to one of what in

[1] Friedrich A. von Hayek, *The Constitution of Liberty* (Chicago: University of Chicago Press, 1960), pp. 224–225.

fact are the benefits, what are the costs? I think that whereas we could agree completely in that formal structure for the analysis, we would for a number of reasons disagree rather substantively on particular policy conclusions.

There are two things that Murray said that I want to address directly. First, I would argue that the Chrysler bailout was in fact a consequence of inadequate regulation rather than a consequence of excessive regulation. The inadequate regulation takes the form of permitting General Motors to have the power position it has in the economy. Were it not for that, Chrysler would not have been as likely to have gotten into the trouble it did.

In the case of the Lockheed bailout, I do not think that there is any way that you could argue that the firm's potential failure was predominantly a consequence of regulation, and that financial aid could be justified on those grounds. It was clearly a case of management betting their company on the Tri Star. That is the nature of the aviation business today. When a firm undertakes to build a new kind of aircraft, you bet the company that you are right. They bet that they were right, and they were wrong on the Tri Star.

My second comment concerns productivity. I would agree with Murray that regulation can reduce productivity as it is usually measured. But that modifying clause is critical. The productivity measures that we usually employ do not fully take into account, for example, externalities, because they are all based predominantly on market value of products and the cost of certain other activities such as the cost of government.

Now, I do not propose to provide any blanket endorsement for regulation. My own work and the work of the Public Interest Economics Center has included very substantial criticism of regulation—not only cartel regulation, which I have attacked over a period of 20 years, but also of some aspects of what Murray calls the new regulation and what I would call social regulation. I would add that whereas one can make both broad and detailed criticisms of the regulatory process as it exists, one can make correspondingly detailed criticism of the market mechanism as it exists (note I do not say equally). So what I would like to discuss now is the nature of the benefits of social regulation, their measurements, and the specific role of information in regulatory practices in the social area. I really am going to make four points. First, I will comment on those areas where additional regulation is, in my judgment, desirable. Second, I will talk in general terms about the need for regulation. Third, I will talk about the nature of the benefits and their measurements. And, fourth, I will discuss the role of information.

There seem to me to be four areas where in my judgment there is a need for an expansion of regulation. The first is in the whole area of antitrust activities. The second is in resource management, the way in which we use our natural resources. The third is in nutrition, and the fourth concerns information. It is so very popular to argue that there is excessive regulation that I think it is important to point out that there are areas where one can, with good reason, wish for still more regulation. The traditional justification for regulation is that there are some kind of market imperfections that regulation can either remove or counteract. The phrase used is usually market imperfection—not, for example, market inadequacy. Imperfection suggests that there is just a little bit of something wrong somewhere. I am more inclined to use the word inadequacy to suggest that there may be more wrong in more places. To begin with, it is rather counterintuitive to believe that the institutionalized pursuit of greed will maximize social welfare, yet that is precisely what economists say in arguing that the free enterprise system is most efficient or the best way to organize social activity. It is true that the "rational" pursuit of self-interest will maximize social welfare under a very special set of circumstances which a century or a century and a half of economic thinking has been able to specify with increasing precision. These conditions are grossly violated again and again in the American economy.

The first and most obvious violation in connection with the social regulation is that the market does a very poor job of taking account of externalities. People who produce and consume processes that contaminate the environment typically do not pay the cost of that contamination. The cost is passed on to other people who must adjust to it. Second, the perfectly functioning market will produce a maximum of social welfare if, and only if, the initial distribution of wealth is optimal. I would suggest that it takes rather a strong mind or maybe a strong stomach to argue that the existing distribution of wealth is in some sense socially optimal.

Third, and this is absolutely critical, the theory of the free enterprise system presupposes the independence of the forces of supply and demand. Now that sounds rather esoteric, but it is an absolute precondition for the free market mechanism to produce the enormous benefits of which it is supposedly capable. In reality, supply and demand are not separate. In the first place, producers, rather than reacting to the existing external objective demand situation, as the theory requires, undertake directly to influence both the supply and demand situation. They undertake to restrict supply through all the cartel regulations to which Murray has alluded, such as import restriction. They undertake to affect demand through their influence on government purchases. In one of my conservative bouts, I was direct consultant to the Air Force Logistics System, and there were more IBM machines in any Air Force headquarters than there were aircraft technicians. The impact that the computer salesman (I can say salesman since it was in the 1950s) had on the procurement process was absolutely shameful. Certainly in that case the independence of supply and demand which is presupposed does not exist. In addition, a very large fraction of business activity is devoted after all to influencing the demand side, to influencing preferences. That is not cricket in terms of the theory of the free enterprise system. Finally, there is a neat little assumption that buyers and sellers have perfect knowledge. I have already indicated that sellers undertake to influence the information available to buyers, particularly through various promotional activities. Furthermore, we live in a high technology society in which it is absurd to believe that consumers can have, at low cost, the expertise that is necessary to make rational consumption decisions. The technology involved does not have to be such terribly high technology. For example, it is very hard to walk into a new house and to make a good guess as to how well the foundation was laid. Now, building inspection leaves a lot to be desired, but it is at least a little better to know that some political hack went through and found out the foundation was laid in accordance with some bureaucratic procedure, than to go in as an uninformed consumer and guess that the foundation was laid reasonably well. The special interest groups that Murray argues are the clientele for much of the "new" regulation have approached the politics of regulation from a position of tremendous disillusionment about the market. Many of their bases for disillusionment may be inaccurate. It may or may not be legitimate, depending on your view of the nature of this society, to charge business with responsibility for anything from OPEC to the war in Viet Nam or the deterioration of center cities. But it is clear that many of the theoretical conditions necessary for the efficient functioning of the market system frequently are grossly violated. Hence, I agree with Murray. We have to have some regulation; you cannot rely on the market to do it all.

Still, in order to make a decision as to whether a particular regulation or a regulatory program is worthwhile, we need to know whether the benefits are worth the cost. Notice that I am saying whether the benefits are worth the cost, *not* whether the benefits equal or exceed the cost. I am saying that primarily because I want to dismiss one argument that muddies the water: namely, the argument that benefits cannot be used effectively in a decision-making process unless they are monetized, unless they are quantified in dollar terms. By and large it is not necessary, in my judgment, to monetize benefits. It is frequently very useful, but it is more frequently unnecessary. What do you need to do if you do not need to monetize benefits? What we need to do is get some idea of benefits by first determining what the effect of the regulation would be. Some regulation is flat out counterproductive—it does not accomplish what it is intended to do; it may even, in some cases, make the situation worse. In any event, one has to ascertain the direct impact of the regulation. Does the regulation reduce sulfur dioxide in the air? Does it reduce the exclusion of people from the marketplace? Does it reduce fuel consumption? What is its direct effect? That is a link that often gets overlooked in discussion of the value of regulation. One assumes that the regulation does what it is supposed to do. Then one has to look at how the society responds to that effect. Is there a reduction in the carcinogen in food? What population is affected? What is the vulnerability of the population? How big is that group? What are their characteristics? And, then, what is it about that group that is affected? Do you decrease their expected morbidity? Do you increase their life expectancy? Do you decrease their sense of alienation? Do you reduce their political dependence—the political dependence of the United States—on Arab oil? What is the consequence of the regulation?

Now, that is where the analysis can end in most cases. The decision maker in deciding whether to insist on a particular action should ideally make some kind of a judgment, for example, that the best available evidence indicates that this regulation will reduce loss of lives due to some particular ailment by perhaps 100-5000 per year. That is about the best range of accuracy you can reasonably expect, one or two orders of magnitude. In the case of saccharin, the estimates of vulnerability to cancer through consuming saccharin range over seven orders of magnitude. We have done all the work, and we say now here is this activity that may save 100-5000 lives per year. We do not need to say . . . and those lives are worth $8000 or $80,000 or $800,000 each. All we need to do is say, is it worth *N* millions of dollars or *N* billions of dollars to increase the prospect of reducing loss of life by that magnitude. The only place where we need to monetize or index in any way is in comparing one program with another. If we have another $10 billion to spend, is it best to reduce the risk of cancer, the contamination of the pristine air of the Far West, or to cut down acid rain in the Northeast? Here in order to make the decision it is highly desirable to have monetary unit. But that monetarization will imply setting a monetary value on very different things. Thus, although monetizing is highly desirable in certain respects, it is unnecessary in most decisions, and is often impossible to do persuasively.

I am an old professor too, and our metabolism is really geared for 50 minutes of uninterrupted pontification. I want to speak about regulation and information, and I want to speak about it in two entirely different ways. One of these involves the notion that regulation can serve as a substitute for the cost consumers would have to incur in acquiring necessary information. An entirely different notion is that information can serve as a substitute for regulation, and regulation, conversely, as a substitute for information gathering and processing by consumers. The major problem is that there is an enormous bias in the information available to consumers about most products. Most of the product information is supplied by the producer, and if management is serious about their function of advancing the material interest of their stockholders, that information is provided in the interest of the supplier, not the consumer. One can accept factual advertising, that is, classified ads stating that something is available at such-and-such a cost. Factual advertising clearly improves performance of the market mechanism. On the other hand, promotional advertising, to the extent that it influences preferences, violates one of the essential conditions of the model for efficient market operation. Thus a great deal of the information available to consumers is, as I have indicated, biased. Furthermore, a number of other promotional activities, stylizing, the content of television programs, which puts a great deal of emphasis on highly materialistic life style, the whole thrust of keeping up with the Jones's—these are all things that influence preferences.

I want to look now at the problem of making consumer decisions in those cases where there are new chemicals that have never before been in the food stream or in a drug supply, or where there are any new commodities with nonobvious characteristics. In these circumstances it is very costly for the consumer to get adequate information for a rational decision. One thing that regulation can do, analogous to the building inspection, is to set a floor under the quality of a product so that consumers can have some assurance of safety. Consumers should be able to go into a restaurant and have some assurance that, even if their preferences for superior quality cannot be expressed monetarily, they are not going to be poisoned. Having worked once long ago in the food industry, I can assure you that if it were not for government regulation, there would be no such assurance. It is extremely difficult to go back and to prove that it was the oyster that gave you what you had. A stock conservative position is that in an economy where participants are committed to a substantial degree of individualism, a great deal of regulation could be removed and information provided. The theory is again based upon this notion that, with perfect knowledge and with the independence of the supply and demand forces, consumers will in fact act in their own interest and that will turn out through the mechanisms of the market to be basically advantageous. I have already mentioned that the available information does not fulfill those criteria. The solution is to give people the information they need in order to overcome the inadequacy of the information available. That makes a lot of sense theoretically, and there are instances where I personally have advocated exactly that. However, in practice, a regulatory agency would have to go through essentially the same hearing process, subject to the same administrative law, in order to come out with a statement that says, "This product has the following hazards." This is, in fact, a direct regulation of the industry, and it is no easier than establishing some quality standard. In addition, it is exceedingly difficult to communicate certain aspects of a hazard. What does it mean to say that if you drink a drink that has saccharin in it, you will run a risk of 2×10^{-6} of catching something. That is not a very easy concept to communicate. Furthermore, if your risk is a function of whether you smoke while you drink while you are taking aspirin, the information becomes very difficult to communicate.

Now, if we think of information as a substitute for government activity, rather than as a form of government regulation, it means that information made available to consumers must be unbiased and balanced. It means that every ad that says this car has the following strengths must say this car has the following weaknesses. You have to have factual advertising. One can envision, for example, a requirement that a brokerage house indicate the fraction of new accounts that made money and lost money last year. This would be an extremely interesting requirement for the commodity brokerage firm where something like 80% of the new accounts lose. That kind of thing is seldom seen in their advertising. An alternative would be funds for counterpromotion, funds for counteradvertising, funds for saying that this new Buick is exactly the same as the last one except that they spent more than $600 to change the design of the chrome.

I would like to conclude simply by saying that I find very questionable both the idea that information can be handled through the private sector so as to preclude the need for regulation and the idea that government dissemination of information can substitute for other forms of regulation. There are tremendous advantages to be gained in providing additional information and providing unbiased information. I would argue very strongly that counteradvertising is a highly desirable activity. I am making no argument that regulation is always appropriate. Some regulation is clearly counterproductive. Some of it is ineffectual. I would argue that many of the regulatory agencies are their own worst enemy. Nevertheless, the question is not whether there are to be regulations or no regulations; the question is what to deregulate, how much, and how.

AN EXCHANGE AND CLARIFICATION OF VIEWS

M.W.: First of all, I like that last set of questions. No doubt, great minds intersect.

A.F.: Even if they are going in different directions.

M.W.: Early on, Allen, you talked about market failure, and here I think the economics profession has done a great disservice to this society, because it views market failure as justification for government intervention. I would argue that market failure, however you choose to define it, is a necessary but not sufficient condition for government intervention. Why? Because we also have to be aware of what I would call government failure. Just as there are all sorts of incompetence in business, there are all sorts of incompetence in government. When I talk about cost—benefit analysis, what I am really talking about is not the green-eyeshade approach, but a way of balancing the good that government intervention would do to correct market failure and the bad it would do in terms of the new sets of government failure that are introduced by providing a mechanism where government bureaucrats can achieve not public ends, but their own bureaucratic ends.

There was a recent federal court decision that stopped OSHA from issuing a new benzyene regulation. It stated, "Although the agency does not have to conduct an elaborate cost-benefit analysis, it does have to determine whether the benefits expected from the standards bear a reasonable relationship to the cost imposed by the standard."[2] OSHA's reaction to that very moderate statement by the judge was to appeal it to the Supreme Court. They do not go along with that approach. This is not unique. Let me read to you from a recent speech, not by an environmental extremist, but the chairman of the U.S. Council on Environmental Quality, the government's own Mr. Environment. He stated, "The immobilizer wants us to overlook the fact that the cost of environmental quality is invariably exceeded by the cost of environmental degradation and that it is the general public who pays the latter while the

[2] 100 Supreme Court, 2844, 1980, *Industrial Union Department* v. *American Petroleum Institute.*

former involve some participation by those who prefer to continue using America the Beautiful as a kind of limitless septic field."[3] I find it very difficult to communicate with people who stand up on their hind legs and take that kind of position. Unfortunately, they are not on the outside griping, but are in charge of the environmental quality activities of the government. The problem that we have, as exemplified by both the OSHA response to the lower court decision and this recent statement of the chairman of the Council on Environmental Quality, is one of rationale in decision making.

On the subject of providing knowledge to the consumer as a substitute for regulation, what we are really talking about is who makes the decision—someone in the government or you? I have recently written about the case of the middle-aged man who, having had a few heart attacks (which means he is very vulnerable to another one), was anxious to use one of the beta blockers. Unfortunately, as he puts it, "I can't use it. My physician is not allowed to prescribe it. Why? There is a remote chance it will cause cancer in rats. I don't give a damn if it is bad for rats. In fact, my life expectancy is less than a year. I am willing to voluntarily take the medicine which over the next 20 years might give me some cancer. I, in my position, want to make the choice, but the FDA won't let me make the choice. They are making the choice for me." That is the kind of problem we are talking about when we compare information versus regulation. Let me suggest (and I think Allen raised a vital point) that you do not want to put a dollar sign on some of these social costs and benefits. Let us instead use the notion of

[3] Gus Speth, Summer, 1979.

equivalents. In the case of the OSHA regulations—benzyene, for example—we are dealing with the carcinogenic equivalent of smoking a cigarette a month. In other words, if you work in this hazardous environment for 40 hours a week, for 50 weeks a year, it's the equivalent of smoking one cigarette a month, or one cigarette a year, or one cigarette in 10 years. You need not put dollar signs on the costs, but there is a need for some rationality. We must offset the attitude of the regulators that zero risk is the goal because modern society cannot operate with that standard. When you give people the opportunity, they do take risks. Zero risk would mean no automobile, no airplane; you simply cannot function in the society with zero risk. Yet the regulators (and sometimes you cannot blame them, because the law is so written as in the case of the Delaney amendment, for example) are in awe of zero risk.

One final point, I enthusiastically endorse Allen's statement about funds for counteradvertising. I am all for counteradvertising, and I think the funds should be fully available. Further, I have a new system for making them fully available without costing the taxpayer a nickel. It is called competition. If you turn on the TV or take a look at a newspaper, increasingly you get comparative advertising. One company is knocking the competition, deflating the exaggerated claims of the competition. That's great, let's keep it that way.

A.F.: I agree fully that the fact of market failure does not mean that regulation is necessarily called for. One has to look at the trade-off. Is regulation in this area likely to be as bad as or worse than the market?—That is the question. If regulation is better, then you'd have a case for it. Clearly market failure is a necessary but not sufficient condition to justify regulation.

Question: I wonder why it has never occured to anybody to let consumers decide how important more information is in the decision, to let them, if it is important, hire someone to inspect the food, to put a grade label on it, to determine it is safe. We have had Good Housekeeping seals around for a long time, and I presume that the fact that they still are placed on some products must mean that some people think it is worthwhile. I guess I resent the implication that I cannot make the decision about whether or not to hire somebody to put a seal of approval on that or not. Some bureaucrat elects to do that for me. I sense that the market really does a better job than you [A.F.] have implied. When my wife goes to buy a turkey to put on the Thanksgiving dinner table, she never looks at whether it is a Grade A, USDA graded turkey. She looks to see whether it has a brand name that she trusts. When she buys peaches in a can, she does not read that can to see what U.S. government grade is on that peach, she asks the question whether or not there is a reliable brand that will stand behind the quality of that peach. I wonder why if all of these information voids are so significant, people have not stepped up and said I don't know what I'm buying and I won't buy it unless there's a brand on it. My point is that I don't think people believe it is as important as you seem to think it is.

A.F.: I agree, they don't. I think that that is part of the problem. First of all, you do in fact do exactly what you said. You do hire people to inspect things and to indicate their quality. So we call them government inspectors and we hire them, we pay them, they do a good, bad, or indifferent job. Some do all three simultaneously. A lot of the food grading, for example, is ridiculous.

Question: But if the damn government grader does not do a good job, I cannot get my money back. If one producer does a bad job, I can go back and say, look give me my money back or I will never buy that brand again.

A.F.: One thing is that it is simply extraordinarily difficult to get the necessary information on some things. For example, take food coloring, people put caramel in bread, with a slight addition of whole wheat flour and the color makes it look as if the bread has a high proportion of whole wheat flour, yet all it really does is change the color and add sugar. There is nothing in the system that provides the information on it.

M.W.: There is something. One of the saddest letters I got in the last few months, was from someone involved in *Consumer Research Magazine.* That is a private nonprofit group that does do, and has done for years, testing of consumer products. They are a very quiet low-keyed outfit that has refused to join the corporate activities or consumer activists crusade. They do not attack companies per se, they just grade and report on tests of individual products. They are, apparently, from this letter, going down the tube. They are not getting the media attention. The activists consumer organizations are not supporting them. They do just what Allen asks them to do, and what probably needs to be done—that is, inspect and report the facts on consumer products. They do not stand up and launch the Ralph Nader–Jane Fonda sort of crusade. The foundations will not support them. The so-called consumer groups will not support them. *Consumer Research* is going down the tube. I think this is very discouraging.

That suggests to me that the so-called consumer groups are not quite so concerned about information for consumers. They do not want the consumer to make up his or her own mind. They want to take positions that result in Big Brother or Big Mother telling the consumers what is and is not good for them.

Question: I am uncomfortable with your [A.F.] decision rule concerning cost-benefit analysis. You seem to imply that decision has to be made at some point on whether regulation is worth it or not, but you're unwilling to quantify that point. I think you and I as individuals can have a subjective opinion like that, but when you set up public policy, you really need to spell out the decision rule you are using.

A.F.: There are two responses. One, I am willing to quantify. I am unwilling to monetize, and those are two entirely different things. In the particular case that Murray mentioned, I would have no objection to a cigarette standard. There is a very clever instrument called quality-adjusted life years. We are trying to index various health benefits by viewing a death caused by some excruciating form of cancer with 2–3 years of terminal horror as being far more serious than an instantaneous painless death from a coronary. You would look at the number of years and the amount of pain. There are various indexes that one might use. They all have the same emotional problem associated with putting a monetary value on these things.

In any event, I said specifically that the decision maker should look at the question from the point of view of balancing the 100–5000 lives with some cost.

Question: But Allen, haven't you at that point implicitly placed a value on life?

A.F.: Yes. Every one of these decisions implicitly sets a value on life, but it's entirely different to do it implicitly than explicitly.

Question: I am not sure I see the distinction between putting a dollar value on life and balancing *N* lives against some dollar cost.

A.F.: I think the distinction is twofold. One, in order to make the evaluation explicit there has to be some kind of a statement that a life is worth *N* dollars. Some people reject that idea simply on moral grounds. You can try the approach of determining what are people willing to pay for a life, but that throws you into the market and the problem of ability to pay! As a result, that becomes politically impossible. It may also be socially immoral to say that we are going to use willingness to pay based upon the existing distribution of wealth in determining the appropriate value to set upon a life. Second, a death is not a death; a year's sickness is not a year's sickness. There is a difference between being really maimed and living for 40 years and having a cold. Even if you have asthma for 40 years, it may not be anything like as bad as being maimed for 40 years. The problems of indexing are impossible ones.

M.W.: Allen, part of the problem is being sentenced to be a bureaucrat. Case in point: Why is practolol, the beta blocker, not approved? Bill Wardell figures that the 10,000 people whose lives would be saved are invisible. The one or two people who would be hurt by the adverse side affects are highly visible. The bureaucrat is concerned about those one or two who would gripe about his decision, not the 10,000 that would benefit, whose lives would be saved, because they are not involved in his or her well-being. I think this cries for some mechanism of balance and I do not mean necessarily dollar signs.

A.F.: I agree, you do not need dollar signs, but you do need to quantify.

M.W.: That is right, and when you are talking about a new pharmaceutical advance that will save 10,000 lives, but will jeopardize 1 or 2, you need decentralized decision making. I do not want anyone in Washington to make that kind of decision. Let the individual physician, with informed knowledge, advise and counsel his or her patients as to the risks and rewards. The guy with two heart attacks should be free to make that choice, not the FDA regulator.

A.F.: I do think that it would be desirable to systemitize the evaluation of costs and benefits by weighing health benefits against health risks. However, don't overplay the one or two FDA mistakes. After all, it has been only 20 years since physicians were handling out barbituates like M & Ms. There are a number of IUDs that had all sorts of adverse consequences. The consequences of the pill were hardly fully explored before it was put on the market. There is no question of the gross errors in regulation; but there have also been gross errors in the decentralized decision.

One can raise the question of whether the United States is singular or plural. Is it appropriate for a person to have a similar set of assurances without regard to whether he or she lives in Alabama or Connecticut? Should unions in Alabama and unions in Connecticut both have the same minimum standards of occupational health and safety, or should there be a difference?

Moderator: Unfortunately, our time has expired, and Allen's last questions will not be answered here, if indeed they can be answered at all. I would like to thank you both for a very lively discussion. If nothing else, it makes clear both the necessity for and the great difficulties involved in establishing coherent and systematic cost-benefit analyses of public policy. It is indeed a great challenge.

CHAPTER **10**

Reindustrialization: A Cure Worse Than the Disease?

JAMES F. GATTI

We OUGHT to act in such a way that what IS true can be verified to be so.[1]

It has become fashionable in recent years to question the long-run vitality of the U.S. economy. Some pundits advise us as to how to profit from the predicted apocalypse; others predict (frequently with great glee) the imminent demise of the private market economy as we know it. One of the most popular remedies proposed for our alleged economic malaise is a substitution of centralized national economic planning for the free market. Proponents differ as to the specifics of their proposals, but support for the general move toward a national plan can be found all along the political spectrum from Ralph Nader and Robert Heilbronner on the left to the National Association of Manufacturers and the editors of *Business Week* on the right. Indeed, behind all the economic reform buzz words like "rein-

[1] Jacob Bornowski, *Science and Human Values* (New York: Harper and Row, 1972), p. 58.

ISBN 0-12-277620-8 0-12-277622-4(p)

dustrialization" and "industrial revitalization" there is to be found some sort of national economic planning. Although the growing fascination with central direction has many causes, virtually all arguments in favor of curing our economic ills by expanding the role of government are based, at least in part, on the phenomenal performance of the Japanese economy in the post World War II period. It has become the accepted wisdom of the media, policymakers, and large parts of the business community that the rapid transformation of Japan from a devastated, war-torn country to the world's third largest industrial power was due to active economic planning by the central government.

In this essay, we will examine some of the arguments and evidence concerning the desirability of public sector economic planning in general and the effectiveness of Japanese planning in particular.

THE NATURE OF PLANNING

It is usually desirable to begin a discussion with a definition of the issue under consideration. In the case of economic planning, that step is essential, for it is only a slight exaggeration to say that there are almost as many definitions of planning as there are individuals with opinions on the subject. In the strictest sense, planning occurs any time a unit makes a decision in anticipation of some future set of conditions. Indeed, under this definition "planning" is viewed as nothing less than a manifestation of a fundamental characteristic of human intelligence, that of foresight. In this respect, Hayek notes that the debate over planning is "simply" one of deciding

> *who* is to do the planning. It is about this question that all dispute about "economic" planning centers. This is not a dispute as to whether planning is to be done or not. It is a dispute as to whether planning is to be done centrally by one authority for the whole economic system, or is to be divided among many individuals.[2]

[2] F. A. Hayek, "The Use of Knowledge in Society," *The American Economic Review* 35 (1945): 520–521.

Although this clarifies the issue somewhat, it also gives the unfortunate impression (which is characteristic of far too many public debates on the subject) that the choice with regard to central planning is absolute rather than incremental. Yet, few people, least of all Hayek, would seriously argue that central planning should be either completely forsaken or universally applied to all decisions. Government seems to be an unavoidable consequence of human existence, and, given its existence, collective decisions must be made which will unavoidably influence the pattern of resource allocation. The provision of those services which are the very essence of government activities—enforcement of the rules of the game, national defense, the odd lighthouse, etc.—affects resource allocation both directly and indirectly. The direct impact occurs when resources are diverted from other uses, and the mix of output changes. Construction of the MX missle system will shift resources away from the construction of private sector housing and commercial space, and to the extent that resources are drawn into the construction industry from other sectors, output in those areas will decline as well.

The indirect effects follow from (*a*) the influence that public sector provision of one particular good or service has on private consumer demands, and (*b*) the influence that the tax structure has on incentives for taxpayers to work, save, and spend. For example, the decision to build the interstate highway system not only shifted resources to the construction of highways away from other endeavors, but also hastened the decline of the railroad industry. Had the interstate network been financed solely from user charges which accurately reflected the true marginal cost imposed on the system by each vehicle, and had both rail and highway systems been taxed in the same manner, there would be no cause for complaint. However, heavy trucks clearly pay less in taxes relative to weight than do lighter vehicles. Because the roadbed must be capable of supporting the weight of the heaviest vehicles, operators of those vehicles are receiving a subsidy from other users. In addition, rail users must pay a price high enough to cover all economic costs plus local property taxes on the right-of-way. Because local governments cannot tax the interstate roadbed, the user fees for the highway system are commensurately lower. Thus, a quirk in the tax structure contributes to the distortion of the relative prices of two important segments of the nation's transportation industry.

Unfortunately, there is no tax system that is both neutral in its allocative effects and capable of generating the enormous revenue requirements of even a "bare bones" level of spending by today's public sectors. The taxation of corporate income to finance public activities is an "easy" source of funds, but the double taxation of income from invested capital may well be retarding capital formation and economic growth by reducing the after tax return to investment. If we tax personal income, added leisure becomes more attractive than the fruits of added work. Alternatively, some of the effort will be shifted so as to generate income that avoids the taxman's bite either because it represents income in kind or is earned "off the books." If we tax spending instead of income, saving will rise. However, it is not clear that artificially depressing current material consumption is better than artificially depressing saving.

The point is not that government activity can or should be made neutral with respect to the private sector. Rather, it is that both the direct and indirect effects of government taxing and spending represent the real costs of public sector activity and must be weighed against the perceived benefits. If this is not done, the well-being of society will suffer. Yet, to be cognizant of them and to act accordingly is certainly to engage in central economic planning with respect to one subset of economic decisions. Unfortunately, that point is often lost on opponents of planning when they categorically reject the concept.

On the other hand, even the most ardent supporter of central planning will admit that the planning for a wide range of decisions must be decentralized and should occur in the "private" sector. Indeed, the current thinking of most planners in the West and growing numbers in the Soviet Union, Eastern Europe, and mainland China is that greater degrees of decentralization (if not "privatization") would be beneficial in those systems presently centrally planned. The experiment with market socialism in Yugoslavia, the official endorsement of decentralization in both the Soviet Union and China, and the stark fact that "private" agricultural plots comprising 3% of Russian land under cultivation produce one-third of its foodstuffs, provide compelling evidence that complete centralization is an untenable goal.[3]

Clearly, then, the issue is neither whether or not to plan nor whether or not to plan centrally. Rather, the issue is to determine the range of decisions that, if centrally planned, will optimize society's welfare. In principle, this requires that individual types of decisions be examined to determine whether or not private or central planning will work best. That determination requires, in turn, an understanding of the conditions under which one system will tend to be superior to the other.

Hayek expressed the limitations of central planning best when he observed that the efficiency of decision making depends upon the mechanism utilized for disseminating the information required. His rationale was that decisions concerning resource allocation require information on relative costs and rewards for different courses of action. Because Hayek believes that the bulk of the knowledge required is highly specialized and specific to "the particular circumstances of time and place," he concludes that it is impossible to centralize the decision and still retain the speed and flexibility needed for timely action.[4] The speed of response is especially critical, as so many opportunities to improve on our resource use (i.e., to earn more profits) disappear quickly, and as the parameters within which one operates change so frequently. To the extent that the response is slowed, the efficiency of resource use declines, and the economic welfare of all of society will suffer as goods are less readily available and then only at far higher prices.

[3] Svetozar Pejovich, "The End of Planning: The Soviet Union and East European Experiences," in *The Politics of Planning*, A.L. Chickering, ed. (San Francisco: Institute for Contemporary Studies, 1976), pp. 107–109.

[4] Hayek, "Use of Knowledge in Society," p. 521.

A bit of reflection on this need for speed and flexibility serves to remind us that in the absence of change, all operations can be reduced to a set of mechanical rules requiring no decisions and, hence, no planning by anybody. The beauty of the market is that it allows so much more flexibility than public sector planning. Government functionaries do not have access to the information that reflects the dynamism of supply and demand conditions and "they will have to find some way or other in which decisions depending on [such information] can be left to the man on the spot."[5]

As noted earlier, this advantage is not ignored by current supporters of planning, and most advocate substantial reliance on the market. Consider, for instance, the two most prominent proposals for increased public sector planning in the United States: the Balanced Growth and Economic Planning Act of 1975 (BGEP), and proposals by the Carter Administration to institute a government directed and/or sponsored program of "reindustrialization" or "industrial revitalization." Supporters of both plans go to great lengths to defend the sanctity of the market for the bulk of economic decisions. In testimony in support of BGEP, Robert Roosa argues that "the need in the United States is not, of course, for a planned economy. . . . What we need is economic planning. . . . "[6] In attempting to develop a meaningful distinction between the two, he essentially argues that under the latter government would do what it is now supposed to do only do it better, that is, with an eye more clearly focused on the future implications of policy action. The only substantive changes in public sector activities that Roosa advocates are (*a*) "an early warning service, capable of locating some, if not all, of the emerging problems"; (*b*) "some focusing on probable long range needs for sustained economic growth . . . to place a spotlight on possible

[5]Hayek, "Use of Knowledge in Society," p. 524.

[6]Robert V. Roosa, "National Economic Planning in the United States," in *National Economic Planning, Balanced Growth, and Full Employment,* Hearings before the Joint Economic Committee, 94th Congress, 1st Session, Part 2, p. 229.

shortfalls in supply"; and (*c*) "tak[ing] the lead in formulating long range goals for the nation."[7]

In a somewhat more specific manner, the editors of Business Week state that

> an effective industrial policy implies a plan and a process for determining which industries are to be encouraged and which are not.
>
> The idea of industrial planning under government auspices stirs legitimate concerns that the government . . . would, in the end, resort to coercion. . . . reindustrialization should not involve a high degree of government planning.[8]

Nevertheless, they go on to argue that some increase in the scope of government planning is essential, if dangerous.

> If the U.S. is to pursue, seriously, policies designed to revitalize its industrial sector . . . the government will have to play a major role in redirecting flows of capital in the economy. . . . A vehicle . . . is needed to channel capital toward ideas and processes that can increase U.S. productivity and competitiveness.[9]

Writing in *Business Week,* Felix Rohatyn maintains that no viable program of long-term "revitalization" is possible without such government intervention.[10] Rohatyn's views are echoed by Lester Thurow, who also rejects detailed planning but feels that broader, centrally established guidelines are essential for long-term vitality. He states

> We do not need central economic planning in the sense of an agency that tries to make all economic decisions, but we do need the national equivalent of a corporate investment committee to redirect investment flows from our "sunset" industries to our "sunrise" industries.[11]

[7] Roosa, "National Economic Planning," pp. 230–231.

[8] "A Solution: A New Social Contract," *Business Week,* June 30, 1980, p. 88.

[9] "A New Set of Priorities for Channeling Credit," *Business Week,* June 30, 1980, p. 131.

[10] *Business Week,* June 30, 1980, p. 134.

[11] Lester Thurow, *Zero-Sum Society,* (New York: Basic Books, 1980), p. 95.

There seem to be substantial inconsistencies in these positions. On the one hand, the sources cited accept the premise that detailed central planning is inferior to the market for most activities; on the other, they embrace it for making major investment decisions and establishing long-range goals. One possible explanation for this contradiction can be found in an observation made by Hayek concerning the nature of information and the relative ability of the market versus the state to convey it. He argues that the choice between using the market and the state

> will be different with respect to different kinds of knowledge; and the answer to our question will, therefore, largely turn on the relative importance of the different kinds of knowledge; those more likely to be at the disposal of particular individuals and those which we would, with greater confidence, expect to find in the possession of an authority made up of suitably chosen experts.[12]

Hayek believes that "scientific" knowledge is more likely to be conveyed best by that "authority" whereas dissemination of all other types is done best by the market. Though not explicitly stated, this seems to be part of the rationale of those supporting central planning for the broader, long-run sorts of decisions facing the economy. The notion that a "national equivalent of a corporate investment committee" is required to channel capital to the potentially more productive sectors of the economy implies that experts with an overview of the entire economy have both superior information and a superior capacity to use it than do the decentralized units in the private sector.

Yet, even here the case is far from clear. Hayek, himself, qualifies his acceptance of the superiority of a central authority for conveying "scientific" knowledge with the observation that one is still faced with the problem of selecting the particular set of expert opinion to utilize.[13] Although he does not follow his line of thought any further, the existence of a significant diversity

[12] Hayek, "Use of Knowledge in Society," p. 521.
[13] Hayek, "Use of Knowledge in Society," p. 521.

of opinion on a particular issue raises the question of whether there is any "knowledge" to be conveyed in the first place. Take the specific case of selecting the "sunrise" and "sunset" industries, to use Thurow's terminology. Will a body of "suitably chosen experts" really posses superior information concerning the specific categories into which a given industry happens to fit? Indeed, will there be sufficient agreement among experts to say with any reasonable degree of certainty that there is "knowledge" to be conveyed? The answer to the first question can be affirmative only if the answer to the second question is affirmative as well.

Indeed it appears that it is the answer to the second question that is the most important, for if there is substantial agreement among a wide variety of experts, the problem will be resolved, at least for the moment. If there is little agreement—if the answer to the second question is negative—then how is one to determine who is correct and which information to convey? It is, after all, the presence of uncertainty with respect to the consequences of a particular change in socioeconomic variables that makes private or public planning so difficult. If there is no (or at least little) disagreement about the consequences, there is no need for planning. Where there is a wide diversity of opinion about the likely consequences of a particular decision, "knowledge" or a singular truth does not exist. Under such circumstances one must conclude that there is no interpretation of a set of information that is sufficiently unambiguous to enable one to impose a particular decision on segments of society that disagree with the interpretation upon which it is based. (It should be noted that the very uncertainty concerning the nature of "truth" is an excellent justification for establishing a political system in which it is very difficult to make and/or change collective tax and spending decisions.)

This problem of knowledge highlights possibly the most important role for the market—the *generation*, as well as dissemination, of information. Essentially under conditions of uncertainty with respect to the outcomes of a variety of alternatives, the set of decentralized actions by independent units serves as a broad laboratory experiment. Individual units will base their decisions on different sets of information, opinion, or intuition. Those experimenters who are successful will be copied by the unsuccessful. The superior information will be ultimately culled from the inferior and disseminated by the market. In the process, the quality of decisions will be improved.

It is in this sense that the opening quote from Bronowski is so apt: We must structure our systems for decision making in such a manner that the best way to do things is most likely to be found.

If energy becomes more expensive, we must allow wide-ranging experiments by individual units to determine the best ways to respond. Governmental edicts such as mandatory mileage standards may concentrate developmental resources in areas where they will be relatively less productive in the sense of reducing the cost of attaining some level of well-being with respect to energy use. These resources might be better utilized in developing new production technologies rather than concentrating on conservation, and only wide-ranging experimentation will be able to reveal which route is most beneficial.

The biggest danger of allowing one central authority (or even several) to plan is that the number of real world experiments is reduced, making their results much harder to interpret. Did a particular technique "work" because of its inherent superiority or because of specific conditions unique to the experimental setting? One or two federally funded pilot projects provide far less information than a market experiment with dozens. A related problem concerns the diversity as well as the number of experiments. Bureaucracies tend to be somewhat monolithic in their view of problems, and diversity suffers. As a result, if a centralized decision is incorrect, the consequences are far more severe than in the case of decentralized mistakes. Fortunately for the U.S. air transport industry, investment decisions are not made by that insightful public body that gave Great Britain and France the Concorde.

An excellent case in point is the recent proposal by the Department of Education that under certain conditions, bilingual education must be provided students for whom English is a second language. To begin with, the costs to society at large of the language barrier have never been established to determine whether and to what extent it is worth correcting the problem with a *public* subsidy. In addition, and perhaps more fundamentally, there is no agreement that bilingual education is the best way to overcome the language barrier and provide the best education in the long run. Many educators feel that bilingual education may only compound the problem. Yet, in its pilot projects, the Department has allowed "only a small number . . . to deviate from the requirements. . . ."[14]

If left to the market, the individual with a dysfunctional language deficiency and/or the individual's parents have every incentive to find the best way to correct it. If a subsidy is still deemed necessary, it should be provided directly to the individual with the problem, and there should be no restrictions on the method of solution. It may well be that the best way to learn English is simply to be forced, during the school day, to use it exclusively. Unfortunately, if the Department of Education has its way, the necessary experiments will not be run, and an entire generation of students will be forced to bear the costs of any resulting mistakes.

Similar arguments can be made about many other attempts of the public sector to extend its "planning"activities to other decisions previously left to the individual. In this regard, it must be recognized that when the market has insufficient information to make the ideal decision, it is not necessarily the case that the public sector has information sufficiently superior to permit it to do a better job. That point has been missed by most supporters of planning.

At this juncture one is prompted to ask about the existence of any evidence that might be capable of providing support for position of planning advocates. The present system has established a record of increasing material well-being and political freedom that is unsurpassed in the history of man. Clearly it is not a perfect

[14]"Perspectives on Current Developments,"*Regulation* (Nov/Dec, 1980), p. 7.

record. The level of performance has varied over time, and certain desirable social goals have not been fully attained. Nevertheless, before alterations in the status quo are carried out, it seems reasonable that proponents of greater central planning should present evidence that such alterations will improve the system's performance. Considering the fervor with which planners promote their cause, such evidence is surprisingly scarce. The favorite example in recent years of the alleged benefits of central economic planning has been the phenomenal performance of the post-World War II Japanese economy.

THE "SUCCESS" OF PLANNING IN JAPAN

The perception that central planning is responsible for Japan's economic miracle has permeated all levels of society. In a widely read book on current U.S. economic problems, Lester Thurow writes, "Japan is marked by a degree of central investment planning that would make any good capitalist cry."[15] This sentiment is echoed by the editors of *Business Week* who conclude that "what Japan's experience demonstrates is that coherent national planning can be a potent instrument for improving a nation's economic performance—to the point, in Japan's case, where it may soon challenge the U.S. for industrial supremacy."[16]

There is, of course, no doubt about the enormous achievements of the Japanese economy since the end of the war. The question that one must ask is whether their extraordinary growth rates can be attributed to central economic planning, and on that point such evidence as does exist ought to cause one to pause before embracing planning as the solution to our problems.

At present, the most systematic investigation of Japanese economic growth is Edward Denison's and William Chung's study

[15] Thurow, *Zero-Sum Society*, p. 7.

[16] "What the U.S. Can Learn From Its Rivals," *Business Week*, June 30, 1980, p. 138.

for the Brookings Institution.[17] In it they apply Denison's standard growth accounting technique in an attempt to establish the sources of Japanese economic growth and determine why the Japanese economy grew so much faster than the rest of the industrialized world. The procedures used to establish the sources of growth, although not perfect, are generally accepted as reasonably accurate and are certainly the best available. Their data indicate that for the period 1953–1971 the average annual rate of growth of Japanese national income per person employed (adjusted for irregular factors) was 8.50% per year as compared to 2.83% for the United States over the roughly comparable period of 1948–1969. The sources of growth for both countries are summarized in eight broad categories: (*a*) exploitation of economics of scale, (*b*) more capital per worker, (*c*) less labor misallocated to agriculture and nonagricultural self-employment, (*d*) changes in working hours and composition of labor force, (*e*) increased education per worker, (*f*) reduced international trade barriers, (*g*) less land per worker, and (*h*) advances in knowledge and miscellaneous determinants.

Items (*b*), (*e*), and (*g*) are straightforward; the rest will require some explanation. The influence of economies of scale is derived from the ability of a growing economy to exploit concurrent growth in the size of the domestic markets by expanding the scale of operations. In many areas, this results in lower unit costs, and permits even faster rates of growth.

The influence of the reallocation of labor is somewhat more subtle though very important. A large, though declining, portion of Japanese labor is employed in low productivity activities (for Japan) such as small-scale agriculture and traditional manufacturing at the level of cottage industry. As labor shifts from these low output sectors to more modern activities, the decline in output in the contracting sector is more than offset by the increase elsewhere.

[17] Edward F. Denison and William K. Chung, *How Japan's Economy Grew So Fast* (Washington, D.C.: The Brookings Institution, 1976).

Changes in average working hours and the composition of the labor force reflect the length of the average work week and the influence of the age-sex mix of the work force. Young workers and women have tended, on average, to be employed in low paying, low output jobs, and relative increases in their participation will reduce growth. Participation rates for both these groups declined substantially in Japan over the period.

The reduction of trade barriers, item (*f*), is seldom mentioned as a potential source of greater economic growth when the issue is discussed in the popular press or Congress. In these forums, the mercantilist perspective of protecting capital and labor from foreign competition still holds sway. Yet, if foreign producers can produce a specific product more efficiently, allowing them to do so will enable domestic resources to be shifted to more productive activities. The total pie is greater and growth rates increase for both trading partners. In addition, the competition provided by foreign producers is one of the single best forces for insuring that domestic firms continually strive for greater and greater efficiencies in the production of existing products and in the development of new methods of providing old services. Nowhere is the importance of this role more dramatically demonstrated than in the case of the American auto and steel industries. Without foreign competition, there would be no benchmark for assessing the efficiency of either domestic industry, and there would certainly be less of an incentive for their respective managements to mend their ways. In this regard, one shudders to think of the consequences of imposing import restrictions on either autos or steel.

The last item, advances in knowledge, is intended to reflect the gains from improved technology, movements along the learning curve, and miscellaneous factors. These particular variables cannot be directly measured, hence this category is calculated as the residual—any growth not accounted for by the previous seven factors is attributed to advances in knowledge and miscellaneous.

Denison and Chung estimated the contribution of each factor for Japan and compared these with previous estimates made by Denison for the United States, Canada, and eight Western European countries over roughly comparable periods. Table 10.1 presents data comparing determinants of growth for the United States and Japan. Each determinant is listed according to its relative importance in explaining Japanese growth. Also presented are differences in growth rate determinants for both countries which permits the sources of differential growth rates to be estimated.

The most striking characteristic of the data is that neither the absolute level of Japan's economic growth nor its superior performance relative to the United States can be attributed to any one factor. The first three factors account for 77.3% of Japan's total growth, the first four for 90.7%, and the first six for virtually all of it. Only the reduction in trade barriers and land per worker appear insignificant. This result is equally pronounced with the determinants of the growth rate differential.

Although the authors do not attempt to do so, it is possible to draw from the Denison–Chung study some tentative conclusions as to the impact of central planning on Japanese growth by examining the relative importance of those growth factors over which the public sector might be expected to have a relatively large influence. In general, these do not seem to dominate either the absolute or differential growth rates relative to their contribution in the United States. Consider, for instance, the category of advances in knowledge. This is an area where one might expect a more centrally planned economy to outperform one that relies more heavily upon decentralized market decisions. Denison and Chung reckon it to be the most important factor in both economies, and, indeed, many individuals attribute a substantial amount of Japanese success to government activities in this area.[18]

[18] See, for instance, K. Bieda, *The Structure and Operation of the Japanese Economy* (Sydney: John Wiley and Sons, 1970), pp. 47–50; Thurow, *Zero-Sum Society*, p. 95; Shigeto Tsuru, "Formal Planning Divorced from Action," in *Planning Economic Development*, Everett Hagen, ed. (Homewood, Ill.: Richard D. Irwin, 1963), pp. 119–149; Merton Peck and Shuji Tamura, "Technology," in *Asia's New Giant*, Hugh Patrick and Henry Roseveky, eds. (Washington, D.C.: The Brookings Institution, 1976), pp. 527–585.

TABLE 10.1
Determinants of Greater Average Economic Growth Rates: The United States versus Japan

	Percentage points			*Percentage of standardized growth rate and growth rate difference*		
Output measure or source of growth	*Japan 1953–1971*	*U.S. 1948–1969*	*Difference*	*Japan 1953–1971*	*U.S. 1948–1969*	*Difference*
Average annual growth rate of standardized national income per person employed	8.50	2.83	5.67	100.0	100.0	100.0
Contribution of determining factors						
Advances in knowledge and miscellaneous determinants	2.37	1.44	0.93	27.9	50.9	16.4
Economies of scale	2.35	0.51	1.84	27.6	18.0	32.5
More capital per worker	1.85	0.40	1.45	21.8	14.1	25.6
Less labor misallocated to agriculture and nonagricultural self-employment	1.14	0.36	0.78	13.4	12.7	13.8
Changes in working hours and composition of the labor force	0.44	−0.34	0.78	5.2	−12.0	13.8
Increased education per worker	0.41	0.50	−0.09	4.8	17.7	−1.6
Reduced international trade barriers	0.01	0.00	0.01	0.1	0.0	.2
Less land per worker	−0.07	−0.04	−0.03	−0.8	−1.4	−0.5

Source: Denison and Chung, *How Japan's Economy Grew So Fast*, p. 54.

It is argued that whereas the bulk of research funding in the United States goes to defense, space, and social services, Japan is said to devote most of its public research financing to economic development, nuclear energy, and general science.[19]

Despite this potential, Japan "outperformed" the United States by only .93% in that area, which explains only 16.4% of the growth rate differential. Had central planning been a major force in accelerating Japanese economic growth, one would have expected this factor to have been a more important contributor both relatively and absolutely.

Similiar observations can be made about the areas of education and trade barriers. Both are within the purview of the "planning" activities of even the most market-oriented economies, yet neither seems to have been a major factor in determining the superior growth. In fact, education is one component where the U.S. economy outperformed the Japanese. Furthermore, Japan has a far more restrictive set of trade barriers than the United States, leaving far more potential for greater gains.

The three remaining sources of growth—increases in capital per worker, changes in working hours and labor force composition, and sectoral labor shifts—contributed more than half of the differential growth rate. In none of the reviews of Japanese central government planning is there any suggestion that the various plans either had or attempted to have any significant influence on them. The plans themselves have been generally referred to as indicative, in that they outline very broad goals for economic performance but establish no direction, either formal or informal, concerning the method of attaining them.[20] Without such direc-

[19] Peck and Tamura, "Technology," p. 567.

[20] See Shuntaro Shishido, "Japanese Experience with Long-Term Economic Planning," in *Quantitative Planning of Economic Policy*, Bert G. Heckman, ed. (Washington, D.C.: The Brookings Institution, 1965), pp. 212–232; Philip Trezise and Yukio Suzuki, "Politics, Government and Economic Growth," in Patrick and Roseveky, *Asia's New Giant*, pp. 755–811; Tsuru, "Planning Divorced from Action"; Tsunehiko Wanatabe, "National Planning and Economic Development: A Critical Review of the Japanese Experience," *Economics of Planning* 10 (1970): 21–51.

tion, planning is at best an exercise in urging the private sector to do its best, a "pep talk" by central government if you will. That approach can, of course, be useful, but it is hardly the sort of centrally directed resource allocation needed to influence capital accumulation, work hours, and sectoral labor shifts, and it is certainly not the sort envisioned by most would-be-planners.

Consider the fifth factor, the amount of capital per worker. Clearly this is a major determinant of per capita income growth, yet nowhere in the discussions of any of Japan's successive national economic plans is there any mention of planning policies designed to influence either the savings rate or rate of investment. Indeed, Wanatabe treats them as variables whose values must be estimated in order to forecast the precise growth rate to be used in the plan. This is hardly the sort of activist planning that seeks to determine the rate of economic growth.[21] Along the same lines, Trezise and Suzuki note "the plans have no binding force on anyone" and, if they work at all, their influence is mostly in creating a stable climate conducive to efficient economics activity.[22] Finally, even Myron Sharpe, one of the framers of the BGEP Act of 1976, feels that Japanese planning falls far short of the type of activity envisioned by that bill. Referring to the Japanese experience, he writes that "Japanese planning . . . leaves much to be desired. . . . A planning commission that makes forecasts to which nobody pays attention is not what we have in mind."[23]

Still, it is possible that Japan's central planners might have had an influence by making the investment that *did* occur more efficient by steering it away from Thurow's "sunset," and toward his "sunrise" industries. This gain in allocative efficiency could show up in either the residual category as an increase in knowledge or in the coefficients on capital output, or both. However, Trezise and Suzuki conclude

[21] Wanatabe, "National Planning and Economic Development," pp. 30–32.

[22] Trezise and Suzuki, "Politics, Government, Growth," pp. 790–792, 808–811.

[23] Myron Sharpe, "The Planning Bill," in Chickering, *Politics of Planning*, p. 9.

> among the nonagricultural industries on which much of the attention and resources were lavished were a number—such as cotton textiles, shipping, and coal—that hardly would have been selected on the basis of growth criteria alone. . . . Some of the favored industries—steel, petroleum refining, petrochemicals, and electric power—had profit rates substantially below the manufacturing industry average during the 1960's.[24]

They further argue that many of the industries aided were more accurately described as declining rather than expanding, and that many of the most spectacular performers in the postwar period were never mentioned in the official plans.[25] They find a similar pattern when they examine the allocation of credit from the Japan Development bank, allegedly a major force in feeding the young and vital industries while mercifully putting the terminally ill out of their misery.

A more complete survey of all the evidence that is inconsistent with the myth of insightful Japanese planning could go on for several chapters at least, but we have neither the time nor the space. The interested reader is referred to the sources cited as a start.

What is striking is the absence of any hard evidence that Japan's superlative performance has been the result of an activist state. The claims that are so often made are simply not substantiated. Such "evidence" as is presented consists of a cataloging of the various activities of the Ministry of International Trade and Industry. These include such things as a "rationalization" of industry by means of merger and noncompetitive cartels, protection of infant industries, licensing the importation of foreign technology, and limitation on foreign investment in Japan. It is taken for granted that these policies caused growth to accelerate.[26] One might better ask whether these policies did not do more harm than

[24] Trezise and Suzuki, "Politics, Government, Growth," pp. 808–810.

[25] Trezise and Suzuki, "Politics, Government, Growth," p. 794.

[26] See Beida, *The Japanese Economy;* Shishido, "*Japanese Experience with Planning*"; Wanatabe, "National Planning and Economic Development"; *The Industrial Policy of Japan* (Paris: OECD, 1972); Eugene J. Kaplan, *Japan: The Government–Business Relationship* (U.S. Dept. of Commerce, 1972).

good. Trezise and Suzuki ask precisely this; they find little evidence of gain and *frequent* instances of likely harm.[27]

CONCLUSION

On balance, the evidence suggests that calls for a greater degree of central economic planning must be regarded with far more skepticism than is currently being shown in many quarters. On logical grounds alone one is forced to ask whether any central decision-making body is capable of generating and disseminating information in the quantity and of the quality that the market can produce. There are good a priori reasons for a negative response.

The experience with planning is similarly poor. The Communist block nations seem incapable of matching the West in efficiency of operations, and the experiments of the United Kingdom are slowly pushing her performance relative to other countries further and further down the scale. Similarly, the evidence suggests that little, if any, of the superior performance of the Japanese economy can be explained by planning alone. The source of her extraordinary postwar growth seems to be simply a matter of doing things better rather than doing things differently. The Japanese economic plans have neither the force of law nor the detail required to alter economic decisions of private units, and to borrow from Mark Twain, reports of its success have been greatly exaggerated.

If a magic elixir for stimulating economic growth exists, it does not appear likely that it will be found in central economic planning.

ACKNOWLEDGMENTS

I would like to thank my colleagues in the School of Business Administration at the University of Vermont for the intellectual stimulation which led me to this topic, Alfred E. Kahn of Cornell University for his insightful comments on an earlier draft, and Robert McIntyre and James Thornton for providing a critical sounding board for my ideas.

[27] Trezise and Suzuki, "Politics, Government, Growth," pp. 792–805.